As we continue to search for an authentic voice in Western worship, the stories in this anthology will give us direction and hope. Jesus is still at work among us and paving the way for His coming with new songs from all over the world.

MICHAEL CARD
author, songwriter, recording musician

At last we have witnesses to the power of music in sharing faith! With supreme devotion to Jesus Christ, and yet little fanfare, the voices in this book have fulfilled the Great Commission through blending Scripture and song in ways that bring cultures and Christ together. This is not the one-way street of 19th century missions, but an exchange of perspectives that gives all of us insight into the myriad ways that God works in the world. *All the World Is Singing* demonstrates that approaching time when Romans 10:18 will be fulfilled: "Have they not heard? Indeed they have; Their voice has gone out to all the earth, and their words to the ends of the world."

C. MICHAEL HAWN
Professor of Church Music, Director, Sacred Music Program,
Perkins School of Theology, Southern Methodist University

Out of each nation's treasury of culture, language and music, the potential exists to craft worship offerings for the Creator, ones that add unique tones and harmonies to the vast orchestra glorifying God. In an age of globalized uniformity, this compilation tells a different story, taking us around the planet with inspiring snapshots of the transforming power of indigenous worship music.

GRAHAM KENDRICK
songwriter, recording worship musician

The secret is out. God is doing a marvelous thing. . . . He is making himself known through song! From the Himalayas to the Amazon with stops on every continent, peoples are joining in the growing crescendo of international adoration of the King of the universe! Fortunato, Neeley, and Brinneman have presented us with an impressive array of worship from around the world. God is gathering all the nations to himself and he is doing it through song. Hang on for an amazing venture. Its breadth will astound you.

ROBERTA R. KING
Associate Professor of Communication and Ethnomusicology

Revelation 7 presents the incredible picture of an international crowd—too huge to count—singing the song of the Lamb. This thrilling read shows that preparations for that great day are already in full swing around the world as peoples and tribes of every tongue 'dwell on his love with sweetest song.'

PETER MAIDEN
International Coordinator for Operation Mobilization

D0596905

Evangelizing the multitudes from every tongue, tribe and people centers on freeing them to worship God and express their faith in Christ in their heart language, music and culture. Yet historically, missionaries too often were not sensitive to this fundamental need of believers from newly evangelized cultures. This excellent reader counters such tactless errors of the Church—and does so in a way that moves us to tears. These stories show how people groups have found new spiritual freedom through mother tongue worship. Get ready to see your heart overjoyed and enlivened at the workings of God. But also expect to be challenged yourself with a deeper desire to worship the Lord of the Nations.

BYRON SPRADLIN
President, Artists in Christian Testimony International
Nashville [Brentwood], TN USA

God gave human beings the wonderful gift of music. It reaches into the internal world of our emotions. When combined with words from Scripture, the Message penetrates to the core of our beings. And when rhythms and melodies from our childhood and culture heritage accent the Truth, the impact goes deeper still. Read these stories, and marvel and rejoice at the power of God's Word, clothed in music from cultures around the world!

JOHN WATTERS
International Director of Wycliffe/SIL

All the World is Singing is a ground-breaking publication and provides, for the first time in book form, a collection of reports of the power of using heart music in Christian ministry from many different cultures and regions. The readability of the text makes it attractive for full-time missionaries and lay people alike. The value of this collection is inestimable and it should be a standard text for any course on missions and music, and required reading for any general course on missions.

TOM AVERY
Ethnomusicology Coordinator for Wycliffe Bible Translators

These stories let us see real faith at work—peoples of the earth wrestling back from Satan the God-given music treasures he has stolen. God lets us take a peek, along with heavenly witnesses, at what is often kept for his eyes and ears alone. As we read these amazing testimonies about creating mother-tongue worship music, may we rejoice together that what had been lost, sometimes for generations, is now being found.

DAVID AND DALE GARRATT
pioneers of the Scripture in Song movement and
presently encouraging people groups to release indigenous worship.

All the
World is
Singing

Glorifying God through the
Worship Music of the Nations

FRANK FORTUNATO

with

PAUL NEELEY and CAROL BRINNEMAN

Authentic

Authentic Publishing
We welcome your comments and questions.

P. O. Box 2190, Secunderabad 500 003, Andhra Pradesh.
www.authenticindia.in

9 Holdom Avenue, Bletchley, Milton Keynes, MK1 1QR, UK
www.authenticmedia.co.uk

1820 Jet Stream Drive, Colorado Springs, CO 80921, USA.
www.authenticbooks.com

If you would like a copy of our current catalog, contact us at:
1-8MORE-BOOKS
ordersusa@stl.org

All the World Is Singing
ISBN-10: 1-932805-81-8
ISBN-13: 978-1-932805-81-9

10 09 08 07 06 / 6 5 4 3 2 1

Published in 2006 by Authentic Media
Reprint, (Revised edition) 2009

Library of Congress Cataloging-in-Publication Data

Fortunato, Frank.
   All the world is singing: glorifying God through the worship music of the nations / Frank
Fortunato; with Carol Brinneman and Paul Neeley.
   p. cm.
Includes bibliographical references and index.
ISBN-13: 978-1-932805-81-9 (pbk. : alk. paper)
ISBN-10: 1-932805-81-8
1. Music--Religious aspects--Christianity. 2. Music in churches. 3. Worship. 4. Church music. 5.
Church development, New. I. Brinneman, Carol, 1947- II. Neeley, Paul. III. Title.

BV290.F67 2006
264'.2--dc22
                                    2006012197

Cover and interior design: Paul Lewis
Editorial team: Megan Kassebaum, Dana Bromley

Printed manufactured and bound in India by
Authentic Media, Secunderabad 500 055

Contents

Solos: The Power of Music in One Life

Symphony
Movement 1: Workshop as Musical Catalyst

Movement 2: Suffering, Persecution, Healing

Movement 3: Church Strengthening

Movement 4: Culture Affirmation

Encore: Reflection and Response

The CD ROM—Bringing the stories to life through photos, audio and video

While the stories of All the World is Singing are complete, they come to life with the accompanying CD-ROM. Included in the media disc are color photos as well as audio and video excerpts from around the world. Some of the music was recorded in a studio by professionals, some outside under a tree, or in a village dwelling on a handheld cassette. Many musical examples, which reflect the aesthetic values from one musical culture, provide a novel listening experience for those from a different culture.

The copyright for the audio and video samples is owned by the composers and/or performers. For other media, it is owned by the person who created it. This compilation's copyright © 2006 is owned by Frank Fortunato, Paul Neeley, and Carol Brinneman. All rights reserved. No part of these media may be reproduced or posted on a website without permission from the media owners. Media may be freely used in meetings, such as classes and churches.

Supplementary media material related to the stories is also available on a data DVD for computer that contain more video, audio and photos. Contact paulneeley@gmail.com for details. Some media is posted at www.worldofworship.org/alltheworld/. A study guide is available for class or small group use. Contact frank.fortunato@usa.om.org to obtain a free copy.

Foreword

Scott Wesley Brown

Paging through *All the World is Singing* is like opening a hymnbook. Compilers Fortunato, Neeley, and Brinneman have collected not lyrics but inspiring and melodious stories that show how God uses song to transform people.

From inner city streets to villages scattered amidst mountains, islands and jungles, a sound is rising around the earth—the glorious expression of hearts released from darkness into light. More ardent than a thousand fires, more powerful than a thousand spears, and more lovely than fragrant flowers, praise is rising, delighting the heart of God. A sound not found on popular western recordings blaring from dashboard CD players, it vibrates through many voices, tongues, and instruments. God hears and appreciates the nuance of every note of praise, whether the music is written in a score or not. In return, He Himself rejoices over His people with singing.

Vast numbers of the world's population are "oral" learners, passing on knowledge through stories. Music also carries accounts from one man's lips to another's. Whether it's through ancient-style chanting or hypnotic rhythms on a log drum, a story is told, a mind is shaped, and another generation carries on the story.

God's people also have a story to tell—the good news of Christ's redemption and healing. The role of the Church includes raising up a generation of new storytellers who reflect God's glory and wisdom among all peoples.

For lovers of Christ, this book will ignite new passion, new vision, new song. May it also ignite the missionary heart of the Church and send men and women forth with the high praises of God on their lips.

This is truly exciting stuff! Open it up and sing along!

Scott Wesley Brown
songwriter, recording musician, and worship leader

Prelude

You hold in your hands something very rare—a collection of stories from the far corners of the planet that documents God's power at work using music within the global Body of Christ. This anthology may be the first of its kind.

In most places of the world, church planters no longer follow the nineteenth century practice of providing new converts western-imported hymn and chorus tunes with locally translated texts. Despite relentless urbanization, the desire to track and connect with one's ethnic roots, including indigenous melodies, rhythms, and instruments, has grown enormously. In recent decades, missions research has enabled the church to recognize this desire, which has naturally increased church and missionary interest in the culture, art, and music of people groups they want to serve. Now the time has arrived to share these incredible stories.

The idea for this collection can be traced to one memorable comment I heard in 1997 at an international gathering of Christian leaders in Pretoria, South Africa. Following my report about the growth of worship in different parts of the world, John Bendor-Samuel of Wycliffe Bible Translators jumped to his feet with a vigorous response to the report. "Here's the experience of Wycliffe in two quick sentences. In areas where translators encouraged new believers to sing newly translated Scriptures, the churches grew rapidly. Where that did not happen, churches grew more slowly."

That's all he said. But as he sat down, I was jolted—emotionally and mentally—out of my seat. Something like fireworks exploded in my brain. It suddenly dawned on me that there was a dynamic and strategic link between a people's growth in Christ and their singing their own Scriptures songs.

At that point I started collecting stories and publishing excerpts of them in an occasional e-zine called *Global Worship Reports.* Many of the stories came from far-off, exotic places where missionaries and musicians—without fanfare or notoriety—quietly fulfilled their calling to encourage people groups to offer their indigenous songs to the Lord. I repeatedly discovered how God kept His people strong in persecuted areas through worship and song.

It did not take much persuasion to get Paul Neeley, editor of *EthnoDoxology Journal* (the only English-language periodical devoted to global worship), on board to assist in the compilation of stories from around the world.

Story after story left us breathless. Watching the *JESUS* film every night for a month had branded the storyline on one man's brain in an African war zone. He ended up writing an epic song on that Luke story. He went from one village to another, singing the story-song and saw more than forty churches planted.

We reread Bruce "Bruchko" Olson's amazing account of how a song about Jesus obliterated demonic activity among the Motilone people group of Colombia—activity that in the past had led to multiple deaths. In that same chapter from his book, *Bruchko,* he tells how one fourteen-hour song about Jesus in the Motilones' language and music style opened the entire group to the Savior.

It was mind-boggling to discover how Estonians kept their faith alive during the crushing Soviet era—almost exclusively through singing. Preaching and teaching had been prohibited, but not singing. Estonians sang their way to freedom!

One Mongolian pastor who was gifted in music and knowledgeable in his culture almost single-handedly initiated an indigenous Christian music movement. While the church of Mongolia, which was comprised mostly of young converts, gravitated to what they knew and loved—worship in a pop western format—God had an equally exciting plan for older Mongolians. He raised up one man to recapture the cultural heritage of a great land and redeem its melodic forms for the kingdom.

Longtime college friend Carol Brinneman offered to edit these exciting stories for this story collection. Carol draws on her African sojourn as a translator with Wycliffe and on her present work of writing and editing at the JAARS Center in North Carolina. She has a knack for finding just the right phrases. She also "rearranges the furniture," as she describes part of her editing routine, and turns the literary equivalent of black-and-white portraits into color-filled pictures, making the stories accessible, particularly to the non-musician and non-missionary. Her friend, mentor, and Wycliffe colleague, Aretta Loving, ably assisted her with final polishing.

Special gratitude goes to Volney James and the Authentic Media staff for their willingness to make these riveting stories available to the general public. Thanks also goes to all those who gave permission to include their stories and articles.

No doubt you will want to spend time at the accompanying websites listed in the final pages of the book to enhance your reading experience by hearing the enormously diverse worship sounds in the body of Christ. Photos and other materials are also available on those websites.

We know of only one mortal who had a peek into the incredible otherworld celebration described in Revelation, chapter seven. God invited John to go behind the curtain of eternity to see a vast gathering of the redeemed human community uniting with the heavenly one at the throne. *The Message* paraphrases the moment:

> "I saw a huge crowd, too huge to count. Everyone was there—all nations and tribes, all races and languages . . . standing before the throne and the Lamb and heartily singing:
>
>> 'Salvation to our God on his Throne!
>> Salvation to the Lamb!'"

That anthem, which encompasses the gigantic mosaic of the world's languages, melodies, rhythms, and harmonies, resides in mystery. No commentator dares tell us if John heard it language by language or all at once in unison. We wait patiently for that time when we too will hear it in heaven. Until that happens, these worship stories from around the world remind us that day by day, year by year, melody by melody, rhythm by rhythm, the great rehearsal is underway, awaiting the time when we join our voices with that thunderous anthem of eternity. Happy reading.

Frank Fortunato
Atlanta, Georgia
November 2005

God as Maestro

Chapter 1

Africa

God Will Make a Way
by Carol Brinneman

In a restrictive African country, three teams of nationals braved travel on bone-jolting roads to reach a remote area to show the *JESUS* film. A few Christians welcomed them, accompanying them from village to village. Using a portable 16 mm projection equipment set, each team showed the film every night for a month—a total of ninety presentations.

The team hoped to find local Christians they could train to follow up new believers and then start worship groups. However, suddenly, a civil war broke out, forcing them to leave extremely disappointed.

Six years passed without any word of the spiritual seeds they had sown. Their frustrations continued, as well as their prayers. Then, one day, a man who had accompanied the teams on the film showings visited the capital city and looked up a national staff person from the project.

Amazed to see the man again, the staff person invited him in. The visitor began, "You know, I was with you that month you and your team showed the *JESUS* film. I watched it every night. In fact, I memorized it."

Reaching into his pocket, he pulled out eighteen well-worn sheets of paper filled with words. They contained the story line of Jesus' life— set to music. He had written a song from the words of the film! It was all there: the Lord's birth, his teachings, his miracles, his death, his resurrection.

In an oral society, such as that of the composer, people have tremendous power of recall, and knowledge passes from generation to generation through stories and music. The man had created a most effective evangelistic tool for his culture. He revisited the areas where the teams had shown the film and began to teach his *JESUS* film song to the people.

He said, "I first taught the song to a few of my people—all eighteen pages. They learned it, and then they taught it to others; it went from person to person and from heart to heart."

Zephaniah 3:17 says, "The Lord your God is with you, he is mighty to save. He will take great delight in you, he will quiet you with his love, he will rejoice over you with singing." God indeed, through his Holy Spirit, passed right through language and cultural barriers and the isolation of that remote region, singing his love and his story into thirsty hearts. The people could not get the captivating tune out of their minds.

The team's long years of disappointment and frustration soon exploded into praise. Seeds planted during their ministry and through one believer's song grew into forty-eight new churches!

In Psalm 2, God laughs at nations that reject his sovereignty. He must also laugh, even scoff, at barriers that threaten to stop the advance of his powerful Word: man-made walls, confusing languages, cultural taboos, political isolation, and geographically remote places. His ways of breaching them astound us, and our hearts can only respond in songs of praise:

God will make a way where there seems to be no way . . .

Chapter 2

Brazil

A Singing Lesson for the Nadëb
by Rodolfo and Beatrice Senn
with Carol Brinneman

Rodolfo and Beatrice Senn admit they are not great singers. "We can keep a tune if somebody leads, but we hardly feel capable of teaching others to sing." Who would show the Nadëb people how to praise God in their own language and music style?

The Nadëb people of Brazil, numbering about 350, live in the northwest Amazonian rain forest. In the fifties, the Nadëb raided small Brazilian river communities, stealing machetes and axes. These incidents resulted in horrific measles epidemics that wiped out most of the population estimated to be around five thousand.

In 1966 an SIL* team, Joe and Lillian Boot, began working among the Nadëb, but health concerns later forced them to leave. Helen Weir replaced the Boots in 1974 and continued until 1995, completing the grammar analysis of the language.

Now the Senns are reaping the fruit of those decades of work. Since the year 2000, most of the Nadëb have accepted Jesus as their Lord. They started worshiping him four to five times a week in a beautiful round church capped with a traditional, thatched roof.

The Nadëb had Scripture to read; they prayed, but they wanted to sing too. A Brazilian pastor had visited the group a couple times and had sung songs in Portuguese. The men assumed his language and style was the legitimate way to praise God. Some of the more outspoken men, including Eduardo, refused to use their folklore music style. They asked the Senns to bring in cassette tapes of Brazilian-style music or another style they had heard sung in the churches downriver. When the tapes didn't come, the men got some from the pastor.

The Senns wanted something better for the Nadëb so they encouraged the people to write their *own* songs. Joaquim, the chief, doubted that singing to Jesus in his own language and style would be acceptable. Nevertheless, he and a couple others found the courage to try—but only on very special occasions. One young man, Tahoi, sang once and everybody laughed. That put a stop to creating and singing Christian songs.

At Easter 2000, Eduardo and some of the men in his family went upriver for two weeks to collect vines. Eduardo felt sad he couldn't spend Easter with the rest of the believers and prayed for comfort. Falling asleep one night, he dreamt he was singing Nadëb-style.

In his dream he saw someone, neither a man nor a woman, dressed in white. Eduardo began singing to this person, "I want to give my heart to the Almighty One." The white-clad person sang back to Eduardo in the same style: "I am the One who is the Almighty One." The dialog continued—a whole dream of a song—Eduardo singing to the One in white and the One singing back to him. The One said to him, "Tell your people not to laugh about their singing. Tell them not to make fun of it."

So vivid was the dream that when Eduardo woke up, he remembered the words and music of the song and wrote them down. When he returned to the village, he taught the song to some of the men. They sang it in the next church service—and no one laughed.

Having received this holy blessing on their own music style, people started writing songs in earnest. A ten-year-old half-orphan boy composed a song that has become one of the people's favorites. Joaquim, chief and church leader, writes most of the songs and uses them as a teaching tool. Before or after a song he explains why he sings it and how the words apply to their lives.

Traditionally, only Nadëb men sang, but women who became Christians began to sing too—with acceptance. Two women, Francisca and Socorro, have composed a few songs. With the help of the Senns, the Nadëb now have a hymnal of fifty songs.

Tahoi, whose singing was initially derided, is now a song leader in church. As he sings before the congregation, praising God in his own language and his own style, everyone joyfully follows his lead.

The Senns no longer wonder who will teach the Nadëb to sing. The One in white has taught them a new song, a hymn of praise to their God.

*SIL International is a faith-based organization that studies, documents, and assists in developing the world's lesser-known languages.

Eduardo, now a church leader, has composed no other songs apart from the one he had in his dream.

When the church was praying about choosing church leaders, God gave Dominguinho, now a leader, a song in a dream or vision saying that it was good to have leaders, but that Jesus was the principal leader.

Some songs are sung by individuals before the congregation. This is cultural since in their folklore dances they always have a song leader.

Progress in the project, as of December 2005: 50 percent of the New Testament is consultant-checked, plus Genesis.

A shorter version of this article appeared in 2005 on the International Council of Ethnodoxologists site: http://www.worldofworship.org/Articles/ArticlesWorkshops/documents.

Chapter 3

Kyrgyzstan

A Church Planted through Songs in the Night
by Don McCurry

A knock on the door in the night. Two young Kyrgyz women ask to come in. They live across the street, heard us singing Kyrgyz songs, and want to listen.

Earlier in the day, our team had piled into two old, Russian Lada station wagons and made the torturous journey over potholed roads to a town of about five thousand—with no church. Seeking out the few believers, we first found a widow. She led us to an elderly couple, and finally, one more was rounded up. Four. That's it. Four old, Russian believers to whom no one ministered.

Once assembled in the couple's home, a talented Kyrgyz man on our team led us in worship, along with our music ensemble that included three other young Kyrgyz men and women and one young Russian girl. We sang in both Russian and Kyrgyz.

After we finished singing, teaching the Word, and praying, the elderly couple prepared our meal. Just as we were beginning to eat, there was that knock on the door, and we invited those two lovely women to join us.

As we finished eating, the young Kyrgyz leader began singing with his team—right at the table. Our guests gladly received the new songbooks we put into their hands. They began to read and then lip-sync the words—words of God's divine love for them. They were completely captivated by the music as we sang on into the night.

Eventually it was time to leave. The women left first. Then we had a final prayer with the elderly Russians and went to our cars, anticipating a long drive home in the dark, rainy night.

But before we could get on our way, the mother of the two young Kyrgyz neighbors came out to the road and stopped us. "Next week, you must come and sing in our home and eat with us," she said.

That night, in the road between two homes, one Russian and the other Kyrgyz, a baby church was born. Hearing our songs in the night, the Kyrgyz neighbors were drawn to music sung in a familiar style, with words in their mother tongue. They could not resist God's message of love for them.

Music, anointed by God, once again displayed its power to draw people to Christ—people of another major religion who probably could not be reached in any other way. Christ knocked on the door of their hearts, and they gladly invited him in.

This is an excerpt from "Tales That Teach," a series of stories, or lessons, gleaned during a long life of ministry in many parts of the world. This project, begun in 2000, is a work in progress. Published copies will be available in the near future by emailing the author at KateBryant@cs.com.

Overture:
Opening Hearts

Chapter 4

Pakistan

Music Opens the Heart's Door
by Don McCurry

From somewhere in the classroom, a well-trained Pakistani voice was singing a beautiful Indian *raga*. I followed the voice. There behind the desk, seated on a small Persian rug, was my esteemed professor, Dr. Daud Rahbar, a Cambridge University graduate, and a renowned scholar and author. Sitting cross-legged, Dr. Rahbar played a pair of *tabla* (male and female Indian drums), accompanied by an electric strumming instrument that imitated an Indian *sitar.* His head was cocked upwards as if listening to some heavenly strain. Out of his mouth was flowing mesmerizing Indian music.

Seeing my look of shocked surprise, he chuckled and said in his whimsical way, "The fool you see seated here on the floor playing the tabla is more real than the stuffed shirt you see trying to teach you from behind that podium."

This self-proclaimed "fool" was to unveil a truth to me that would open up many hearts to God's Word.

As a missionary in Pakistan, for four and a half years I had wrestled with local theologians over theological issues that divide their religion from Christianity. I knew I needed to gain a knowledge and appreciation for many other aspects of Pakistani life and culture.

Therefore, as we returned to the States on furlough, I had asked God to arrange for me to study with a convert to Christianity, a Pakistani PhD in the area of Urdu Literature. There was only one: Dr. Daud Rahbar in the Kennedy School of Missions at the Hartford Seminary Foundation. God answered my prayer.

The singing encounter in the classroom was only one of many delightful experiences I had as I worked on a Master's degree under this gifted teacher. Dr. Rahbar led me through a study of the great Persian masters: Firdawsi, Amir Khusrao, Hafiz, Sheikh Saadi, and Omar Khayyam. Then we plunged into Urdu poetry. We studied the poems of Vali Mir, Dard, Sauda, Insha, Ghalib, Atish, Zauq, Momin, Anis, and Dagh. These names may mean nothing to you, but for me, they opened up vast riches of the cultural heritage of people in Pakistan and India.

Studying Urdu literature under his supervision turned out to be one of the most pleasurable and profitable periods of my missionary career. Later, it enabled me to move comfortably among the poets and prose writers of Pakistan, some of whom became my friends.

Of all the valuable insights Dr. Rahbar shared, one stood out from all the others. I don't know if he understood what a bombshell of an idea this was for a missionary. This is what he said: "Don, you can say anything you want—in poetry or music—to these people and they will receive it, but if you preach it in prose, they will probably try to kill you."

After returning to Pakistan, I put it to the test. I had been chosen to be Summer Pastor for the mission community in Murree. After gaining a promise of support from musically talented missionaries, I went to the mayor of the city and asked permission to stage an international music festival. He allowed us to take over an abandoned roller skating rink.

We presented a program of folkloric and religious music from thirteen countries. Performing midpoint in this two-and-a-half-hour program was the best Pakistani Christian singing ensemble in the country. Their message was thoroughly biblical and pointed to Jesus Christ as Lord and Savior. The audience clearly heard the gospel.

When the curtain closed, everyone in the audience was standing and heartily applauding. The mayor then made a little speech. He said, "This is the greatest social event that has ever been staged here in Murree. We hope you who are guests in our country will come back and do this every year." I couldn't believe what had happened. Our friends had sanctioned the whole gospel—in music.

Dr. Rahbar knew what most missionaries never learn. These people are forbidden the use of music in worship for, too often, music is associated with prostitutes and dancing girls. As a result, they are starved for music.

Eternally grateful for this lesson, I have taught it to generations of missionary candidates. In God's wisdom, seemingly weak means, maybe even "foolish" ones, prove to be powerful communication tools in opening the door to hearts: poetry and music.

An excerpt from "Tales That Teach," a series of stories, or lessons, gleaned during a long life of ministry in many parts of the world. This project, begun in 2000, is a work in progress. Published copies will be available in the near future by emailing the author at KateBryant@cs.com.

Chapter 5

Thailand

What Happened
After Grandma Danced

by Paul DeNeui

A voice called out, "Grandma, *sit down*! What do you think you're doing?"

Without a break in her motions, she simply stated, "You don't tell your old grandma to sit down. I'm ninety years old, and I'm just thanking the Lord that you're here."

During an Isaan language Bible discussion in Thailand, as people sat on straw mats in the home of a believer, one elderly woman stood up from her squatting position, stepped into the middle of the circle and suddenly began to dance traditional Isaan steps. Her thin arms and fingers waved gracefully back and forth in rhythm to her small, delicate steps. It was a familiar sight at drunken parties—but this was *Christian worship*! There was no music, only a stunned silence.

Jesus is a foreigner in Thailand. Thai Christians use primarily Western imports to worship Him. The average Thai, viewing church practices throughout the country, would say that Christianity is the foreigner's religion—the Westerner's way of gaining merit. Most Thai reject Christianity and choose to follow another religion, an integral part of their national identity.

But what would happen if Jesus came to them as a Thai? What would he look like? How would he talk? What would he eat? What music would he enjoy? What would happen if John 1:14—"The Word became flesh and made his dwelling among us"—became a reality for Thailand today?

The northeast sector of Thailand is home to approximately 20 million people known as Isaan. With a strong Lao heritage, the majority of Isaan are culturally different from the central Thai: their language, their diet, and their musical heritage, which goes back hundreds of years and remains popular today.

Jim and Joan Gustafson went to this region as missionaries with the Evangelical Covenant Church of America in 1971. By God's grace, they helped the people encounter Jesus as if he were one of them. The Word was reborn as a northeastern Thai.

Simply using the local language in worship made an immediate impact. Isaan believers exclaimed, "Jesus talks *our* village talk!" This was, and still is, a radical concept. Unfortunately, even today, thirty years after the Gustafsons' arrival, most Westernized Thai churches in the Lao-speaking region of northeast Thailand still use the central Thai language in their worship.

After Grandma danced, however, everything changed. Traditional dance became a part of worship. And music soon followed.

Isaan culture has a variety of beautiful, melodious indigenous musical instruments. None, though, expresses the peoples' heart more than their bamboo mouth organ, known locally as the *kaen*. Incorporating the kaen into worship, however, did not come without questions. In animistic practices, the kaen is used to call upon the spirits. Was it appropriate to use the kaen to worship the Lord Jesus Christ?

Thai Christians still debate its use. Some cannot separate the idolatrous practice from the instrument, and therefore condemn the kaen as "satanic." However, for Isaan people untouched by Western religious influences, the kaen remains the sound of "our people." It speaks deeply to the heart of Isaan who are now in a new family as God's children.

As one follower says, "Why can't we use the kaen to praise God? Before we became Christians, we used our mouths to follow spirits. Does this mean we now need to get a new mouth to praise God? Isn't a new heart enough?"

Gifted men and women, changed by the grace of God, have produced a complete hymnody of Isaan music, and they continue to write more. The church has truly become an indigenous Thai Isaan church that rejoices in using the best forms from their culture to celebrate new life in Christ. One recent song, translated below, declares that Jesus is no longer a stranger to Isaan people. And when Isaan Christians sing it, they get up and dance!

Join in Praise

Lyrics from an Isaan worship song:

From the Heavenly City the Word came down.
He was born right here where we live.
We Isaan people have new happiness now.
He loves us and that will not change!

From the City Above, he came down for us.
Full of love from the Almighty.
Now listen! The sound of the *ching* and the *kaen,*
And who is that playing the pin?
Hear the clear tones of the *ponglong* as they join
The sounds of the saw, "Eeee oon aaaw."
The melody of the saw is coupled
With the sound of voices of praise.

The Lord Jesus Christ, the Victor over death,
Is born in our cultural forms.
Listen to the sounds of the flute and the drum
All Isaan rejoices in Him!

This is adapted from an article originally printed in *Mission Frontiers,* June 2001.

Chapter 6

Burkina Faso

Once Again They Dance by the Light of the Moon

by Aretta Loving

"It's like the old days when we were children! Young people used to play music, entertaining the old folks, under the light of the moon."

On hearing such comments from many older people, Pastor Josias Djenné responded with, "Yes! These new Bissa songs have encouraged us. In our church, some don't understand the 'foreign' songs, especially the older people. But when we sing songs with the calabash,* even the old people come to church. And they understand God is alive because they listen to the music."

For many years, Pastor Djenné had desired to see his Bissa people of Burkina Faso, West Africa, reached with the message of God's Word. "I was especially concerned for the elderly," he says. "Now this new kind of Bissa music is impacting our whole community." Delighted with these evening "concerts," this Assembly of God pastor's voice reflected almost childlike enthusiasm.

Along with men from four other churches in the Bissa area, Pastor Djenné had worked with Ruud and Connie Hidden of Wycliffe Netherlands to translate the Bissa New Testament. Ruud says, "Right from the beginning of the project in 1979, we cooperated with local government agencies to develop an alphabet and to set up a literacy program in Bissa."

Despite that literacy program, once the New Testament was published, a large segment of the Bissa population was not able to read it—mainly those "elderly" for whom Pastor Djenné was concerned. In 1998, as he held in his hands a computer-generated copy of the New Testament, he wondered, *How can we reach the older people since they rarely leave their homes?*

As he wondered, a young American lady became part of the solution to his dilemma. Mary Hendershott, a Wycliffe ethnomusicologist, regularly holds music workshops with different language groups in Burkina Faso. That year Mary held a music workshop with the Bissa people. At the workshop, Scripture songs using Bissa song styles set to traditional music were composed by the participants.

"Up until then," Mary says, "the Bissa church had used French hymns or music borrowed from a larger, nearby ethnic group. This 'new' music not only uses the heart language of the Bissa people, it also uses their heart music. I was elated as I listened to Pastor Djenné's enthusiastic report on what has happened . . . ."

"Since that workshop," Pastor Djenné begins, "our people now hear our own music—Bissa music—and young and old gather to listen." Then with a broad smile and eyes alight, Pastor Djenné claims, "This music deeply touches the hearts of these elderly ones! They hear the message as well as the music."

And not just the elderly listen. Bissa people of all ages are excited about this new thing that has become a part of everyday life. "People sing these new songs in their homes. As they work together—in their fields or building houses—they sing them. They walk down the street singing them. People who haven't yet believed in Jesus hear and take note. Some now come to church just to hear the music."

Recently Mary returned to help with another workshop. She was greeted with the news that "many of our Bissa people have listened and come to the Lord." One person reported, "The people love these songs! When we drum the melodies with the calabash, people cannot just pass on by."

Someone else added, "One evening the chief and all the elders started *dancing* right out in the chief's courtyard. They wanted us to play the music all night long."

Pastor Djenné concludes, "This new way of worshiping is here to stay!"

In 2000, the Bissa New Testament was sent away for publication after Pastor Djenné and others did a final read-through. Church representatives signed a letter approving the translation and pledged to do all they could to facilitate its use in the churches. "That was a joyful moment for Pastor Djenné and for all of us," Ruud says.

Today Pastor Djenné preaches to his congregation from one of the ten thousand published Bissa New Testaments. As he does, he notes with praise to God the number of elderly people there—because, "They listened to the music!"

---

*The calabash, a large gourd, is also called bottle gourd, or squash gourd. The Bissa people cut the calabash in half, dry it, then make it into a musical instrument. It is turned upside down on the ground and tapped or beat on with the fists.

This story has been translated into Dutch and appears as a chapter in *Zoeter dan Honing*, published by Wycliffe Bijbelvertalers Nederland. It will appear in *Together We Can! A Mosaic of Stories and Devotions Displaying the Impact of God's Word*, by Aretta Loving, to be published in 2006.

Chapter 7

Brazil

"How About That! That's *Our* Song."
by Pat Ham

An old woman came up to me and said, "What's the matter with you? You have been here all this time, and you haven't given us a single song! And here this man, Tomas, comes to visit us for only two weeks, and he leaves us with all these good songs. What's your problem?"

This was the first verbal spanking I'd gotten since working with the Apinayé* people of northeastern Brazil. But it showed me—albeit painfully—how much the people accepted and liked the new songs that ethnomusicologist Tom Avery helped them create.

If you go to an Apinayé village dance and say, "Tell me what you're singing," they will probably say, "I don't know." Apinayé cannot understand the words of about three-fourths of their songs. Very few have only Apinayé words. They are a mixture of words from neighboring languages: Canela, Kraho, and Krinkati. A few of the older people who have sung the songs a long time and understand more foreign words might be able to tell the meaning. The result is something like the song I used to sing when I was a teenager:

Mairzy doats and dozy doats, and liddle lamzy divey

A kiddley divey too, wouldn't you?**

You can understand some of those words, but it doesn't quite make sense.

According to legend, an Apinayé hero named Pẽẽbixit was the foremost song writer. When Pẽẽbixit saw something unusual as he walked down the trail, he would write a song about it. For example, he might see a little alligator in the river. Then another animal might come and steal the alligator's food. Pẽẽbixit would think, "I'll make a song out of that!" That could have been the origin of this one-note Apinayé song:

Mĩti kuxyre	Smelly alligator
Têrê hkupe	From him
Nhõ mry krẽre	His food was eaten
Mĩti kuxy	Smelly alligator

The song repeats these words over and over.

Or Pẽẽbixit might see a certain type of monkey with big ears. He'd say, "Ha! That will make a good song!" That might have been the inspiration for the following song, which has two notes:

Hê ja kupytytêre	Look at that monkey
Jamaky jakotore	Ear wide
Hãy hãy hãy	Hey, hey, hey!

Apinayé sing these words two or three times, then instead of singing about the monkey with the wide ear, they sing about something else with a wide ear. These songs about nature are the only known Apinayé songs, and they've been around longer than anyone can remember. No one ever made up new songs.

Then Tom Avery, with son Matt, came to stay with the Apinayé for two weeks in 1992. Before Tom left, he gave them a cassette tape with eighteen different hymns. Since he had previously done an analysis and hymn-writing project with the Canela, and saw the similarities to Apinayé songs, it was decided to simply adapt the Canela hymns to the Apinayé language. The Canela tunes for these hymns were already familiar to the Apinayé. And they could understand the words; every single word makes sense—very good sense. Apinayé avidly listened to them.

When Tom came, I had no idea what sort of reaction there would be. I didn't know whether they would laugh or say, "Oh, we don't want songs about God. We have our own songs." I was overjoyed with such enthusiastic acceptance.

I made about a dozen typed copies of the songs for Apinayé readers, and these song sheets quickly became a great prestige item. Every night we would play the tape Tom had made, and readers were invited to follow along on the sheets. Anyone who could read just two or three words was considered a reader with the right to come up and take one of the sheets. Song sheets became a great help to new readers. Even slow readers were able to read along as they listened to the words on the tape, and their reading skills rapidly improved. Night after night, Apinayé came to sing.

Our language assistant's son, Joshua, in his early twenties, was extremely excited about the songs. After Tom had left, Joshua changed words to some of them and added many more verses to others. Then he wrote five songs himself! He took the Canela hymn tape that Tom had left with me, listened to the music, and made up new songs. Instead of just eighteen hymns, they then had twenty-three. The Apinayé especially liked Joshua's songs.

One of Joshua's songs says:

> This book, take this book.
> It's God's Word; read it well.
> This is our book.
> This is our book.
> Let's sit, reading it well.

Another song says:

> Let's follow God's Word.
> Let's follow God's Word.
> And let's sing to him the good songs.

Joshua's enthusiasm made the young men and teenage boys feel it was okay to sing the songs too, and they started coming to listen. One week, for several nights in a row, some teenage boys would leave the village TV or other group activities and come to our porch, take the song sheets, and sing along with the tape.

Down at the creek one day, a little girl said something about climbing a nearby tree. "That's a tall tree," I said. "If you climb up to the top of that tree, you will almost be up in the sky."

Her face lit up as she replied, "God's in the sky. That's one of our songs: 'God is sitting in the sky. He's watching us.'"

One afternoon, I heard children singing outside. I went out and saw they had hung a hammock and four little ones were stacked up in it together. They were swinging back and forth as fast as they could, singing, "God created the heaven, God created the earth, God created the animals, God created the Indians." Apinayé legends don't say that; legend says that the sun and moon created everything, including the Indians. But now they have a song that says God did it—and they're listening.

Before these new songs came, if I had asked a child, "Who made the animals?" or "Who made the Indians?" he would have responded, "I don't know." Most Apinayé don't remember their legends anymore. But now, things are changing. One day, some children and I were walking down the trail. I said, "Look at that pretty flower! Who made the flowers?" They replied, "God made them." I said to some other children, "Tell me about heaven. What's God's village like?" There is now an Apinayé song about that. The children said, "Oh, God's village is really good!" They know this because of the songs.

At this point in Apinayé history, music is a much stronger, more effective vehicle of spiritual truth even than the written word because music is already part of their culture. The written word is a new thing they have to learn about. It will take a long time before we have enough Scripture*** for them to be able to read about the truths they're already singing.

Before I was to leave the village for a few months, the older women would come and sit with their ears right beside the cassette player, concentrating on learning the words to the songs. They wanted to be able to sing them after I left, and they were very carefully printing the words in their minds.

When I returned months later, the children saw me coming and shouted, "Here comes the lady that plays the hymns about God!" The house was packed with people wanting to hear the songs. Now at least one Indian in every Apinayé village has a battery-run cassette player so that each village has the songs available to them. Many are now singing the songs about God's Son, Jesus, who died for us and came alive again, and their hearts are responding.

One day, a three-year-old boy saw my cassette player on the table. His eyes lit up, and he climbed on the table and sat waiting. When nothing happened, he began to cry. I asked, "What's the matter, Tembrex?" In a tearful voice, he said, "Jesus!" He wanted to hear the tape about Jesus.

Many Apinayé responded to the Lord as they heard about him in this powerful way. They seemed to feel the words in the songs were inspired. Because these were their own Apinayé songs, they felt they needed to listen to them.

One night after listening to the tape for a while, a woman turned to her daughter and said, "That song says we're supposed to follow God's ways. How about that! That's *our* song telling us to follow God's ways."

Epilogue

In 2005, Brazilian missionaries with New Tribes Mission helped the Apinayé produce a CD of more new hymns.

---

*The Apinayé are hunter-gatherers and agriculturalists; their population in 2005 is over one thousand (Ham).
**Words and music by Milton Drake, Al Hoffman, and Jerry Livingston.
***The New Testament was published in 1999.

This article is adapted from "Sing to God the Good Songs," which appeared in *EthnoDoxology,* 1:3 (2002), pp. 14–16.

Chapter 8

Senegal

Chanting the Gospel of John:
An Experimental Approach
by Sue Hall and Richard Shawyer

"Give me some peanuts!"

"No! These are mine. You've had yours."

"Will you children stop that noise and just go and play somewhere else?"

The grandfather handed over some more peanuts, and the children scampered away, leaving the group of men in peace. Sitting on mats under the shade of a tree, the men listened to the tape player, while mint tea bubbled on the charcoal stove. All ears were bent on the chanted message coming from the speakers. No interruptions would be tolerated because this was clearly a message of great importance. The melodic flow of the solo voice told of the Word of God entering into this world, bringing light into darkness and power from God that had never been seen before. *Who is this Word?* they wondered.

The missionary stopped the tape at the end of chapter two of John's gospel, and moved into the Bible lesson for the week—teaching through stories and questions.

The following week, however, he discovered that the stories that really stuck in the minds of those listeners were the texts—chanted in the same form as those from their own religious book. Their preference for oral communication helped them retain the important, new messages and recall them a week later, without prompting.

Chanting Scripture is one of many techniques used to encourage people to listen to and accept the Bible. Although it may not be appropriate for all contexts, this example shows that in certain places the medium of chanting can be helpful. The concept and planning of this trial project was done by a group of Christian workers reaching out to one large ethnic group in the interface between Arab North Africa and black West Africa. This group has resisted the Christian message for decades, especially since the gospel has often been presented in "foreign clothes" and seen as irrelevant to this self-confident and proud people group.

As Scripture is translated into the local language, the challenge is to see it reach the ears of those who most need to hear its message. A partnership of media specialists is working to see suitable products developed. They discuss what products would serve best, such as print or non-print media; dramatized or simple readings; musical accompaniment or songs.

One yet-untested possibility was to present Scripture through chanting. A decision was made to record John's gospel in the local language using an adapted chanting style normally used for reading the people's religious book.

One of the few local believers had been trained, as a student and during his pre-Christian years, to recite lengthy passages. This skill was recognized by a missionary working in his area, and the man was asked to try reciting Scripture from the printed New Testament in the same way. The results were pleasing to other believers who heard his chanting of the Christmas story.

To share Scripture more widely and test out people's reactions, the media group decided to make a simple recording of this man's recitation. The recording, made in 1999 in a local Christian studio, often captured a whole chapter or more in one take so not to disturb the flow of the text. In the final tape processing, some echo was added for aesthetic enhancement, which local people preferred. Most recordings of religious chanting sold in this area have a high degree of reverberation due to the size of the place of worship where they are recorded. Care was taken, though, not to add too much echo because the quality of most cassette players used by local people is not good, and recorded sounds are easily distorted, which will, of course, affect what people hear and understand.

The final recording product is a set of three sixty-minute audiocassettes that have pauses (for turning the tapes) in logical places. The cassette cover format is simple but reflects designs used for religious literature in the region, with text presented in Roman and Arabic scripts in the local language to maximize comprehension.

Through the efforts of a group of Christian workers, these tapes are spreading across the area, taking the message of John to ears and hearts that would never pay attention to it in another style of presentation. The chanting style demands serious attention—for a serious message.

Solos:
The Power of Music
in One Life

Chapter 9

Pakistan

Two Blind Men
by Don McCurry

The very appearance of the blind man was a challenge to my faith. There were no eyeballs in his sockets. Skin had grown completely over the hollow areas where his eyes should have been.

Could Jesus heal this man? I wondered. *After all, in his own lifetime, Jesus healed a man born blind. Surely, nothing was impossible with God. Jesus could do this.*

As newly arrived missionaries in Pakistan, we spent our first summer in language school, living at the missionary station near the town of Murree. Walking two miles to school every day and following the curving mountain road, we marveled at the beauty of the countryside.

Invariably, when we neared the center of town, we encountered the blind man. You couldn't help but notice him. So many times I wanted to stop and talk to this man. My heart was bursting with faith to believe the Lord could heal him—give him new eyes where none existed before.

But I was mute. I had to learn the language first.

Other missionaries noticed him too. We learned his name: Kalu Khan. He was a member of a major religion. He lived nearby in a hillside village and frequently came into town.

One day, a missionary friend who could speak the language talked to him about Jesus. "Even in your religion's book," my friend said, "it is written that Jesus could heal the blind." Then my friend asked permission to pray for him in Jesus' name.

Kalu Khan cursed him, in response. "You are a *kaffir* (an ungrateful blasphemer)," he said, "and you are going to hell because you believe Jesus is the Son of God."

When I heard this, I asked myself, *Why does he react this way?* In truth, his response served as a quick introduction to his religion. Its founder pronounced a curse on everyone who believed Jesus was the Son of God.

Comparable words from the Bible came to my mind: "Cursed is the man who leads the blind astray . . . " (Deuteronomy 27:18). My heart grieved for blind Kalu Khan.

Daniel Maseeh, born in a Christian village, was also blind. Blessed with a beautiful voice, he had learned, since childhood, many psalms and hymns. Daniel had another gift—a heart for evangelism and teaching. But he found it hard to bend the familiar psalms and old time hymns to his purpose.

Eventually he discovered *kuwwali*, an indigenous form of Indian music that grew out of a style commonly used by *Sufis* or mystics. A medium for expressing devotion to God, it employed antiphonal singing. The lead singer, usually playing a harmonium, would sing out a line, and then the other singers would lead the audience in singing the line back in response. This was easily adapted as a way of teaching—storytelling through music.

In the agricultural year, seasons of inactivity proved ideal times for a good Christian Punjabi sing-along. Such was the time I first participated in one of Daniel's all-night kuwwali songfests. In a Christian village near Faisalabad, we sat on reed mats in a large, open courtyard. The village sounds filled the air: buffalo, donkeys, camels, barking dogs, and playing children—until Daniel began. His melodious voice filled the night air. Beginning with Adam and Eve, he taught through music. We learned to sing the epic stories of the Bible. It was a perfect communication technique for people who could not read, or could read only a little, for children—and for me.

When Daniel got to the miracles of Jesus, he sang:

And Jesus made the blind to see.

And the audience responded:

And Jesus made the blind to see.

I responded too—with tears—aware of the great miracle I witnessed. Daniel was blind, but he saw. He saw with the eyes of faith. He saw Jesus. Jesus had totally healed him, inwardly. His soul radiated the light of the indwelling Christ as he sang:

> *The night of my sins was washed away.*
> *The light of Christ has come to stay.*

Kalu Khan and Daniel Maseeh: two blind men, but one could see.

An excerpt from "Tales That Teach," a series of stories, or lessons, gleaned during a long life of ministry in many parts of the world. This project, begun in 2000, is a work in progress. Published copies will be available in the near future by emailing the author at KateBryant@cs.com.

Chapter 10

Siberia

Love in Siberia:
A Musician Friend for Life
by Robin Harris

At the last Sunday worship service before departing Siberia in 1998, I sat in a rickety front-row theater seat, wondering, *When is the Lord going to send me a Sakha musician friend?*

For months, I had been praying for a friend who loved traditional music—ever since I myself had come to love the music of the Sakha, a Siberian ethnic minority. I was leaving for a year to begin graduate work in ethnomusicology, hoping that training would enable me to encourage Sakha people to use more culturally-appropriate music in their churches.

Our church, a sagging wooden structure that was slowly losing a gravity war to the melting permafrost beneath it, reflected many other Sakha churches. They had sprung up after the fall of communism, yet most believers sang only Russian-style songs in order to accommodate their Russian brothers and sisters in the Lord. Even more distressing, many people viewed traditional song styles as being "less Christian" than the Russian-style songs.

Lord, if you could send me just one friend that cared about Sakha traditional music, someone who could model the appropriate use of traditional styles in worship, it would make a huge difference in Sakha attitudes toward their heart music, I mused.

For the past three years, my husband Bill and I had worked with a Russian and Ukrainian church-planting team to start this church. It had grown to the point where our rented hall was so full that the young people stood at the back, leaving the seats for the women, children, and older people.

Roughly a third of the congregation was Sakha, paralleling their population percentage in the city. We had encouraged the Sakha to express themselves in culturally significant ways in church, and they had grown increasingly comfortable with publicly praying and singing in their own language. To their credit, our Russian brothers and sisters had developed a heightened tolerance for using the Sakha tongue in the worship service. But because of the ambivalence toward Sakha song styles, Russian songs still dominated the worship service, even though many of them had been translated into the Sakha language.

My mind still on the musical challenges, I heard the Russian pastor announce that we would be leaving for a year. He motioned for us to stand and speak.

How are we going to explain that we're leaving so I can attend school? Russians don't go to school at our stage of life!

With our two children at our side, Bill and I took turns saying our goodbyes and explaining that we were leaving only for a year to get training—we would be back, hopefully better equipped for our work.

For the first time, I talked publicly about my interest in Sakha traditional music and my hopes that new, Sakha-style songs would someday be written and used in church. Although I had this desire, I didn't know how to help others achieve this, so I was going to America to learn more.

As the room slowly cleared, a Sakha woman about my age came to talk. She shyly introduced herself as Luba, the shortened form of the word meaning "love" in Russian. Her excitement soon overcame her timidity and she said, "You love Sakha music!"

"Yes!" I answered enthusiastically.

"I am a new Christian, but I strongly desire to sing real Sakha music to the Lord. I had no idea there was anyone else that felt as I do. I teach folklore and traditional song at the College of Culture in this city. It is a very difficult place for a Christian to work, but I think it is important to be a witness there."

Thank you, Lord, for your answer to my prayers! I left the service convinced the Lord was at work; my ministry had turned a corner.

That Sunday was the start of my close friendship with this gifted Sakha woman. As we parted, I told her that the most important thing for her to do was to grow and become mature in the Lord. She would thus gain credibility in the eyes of other Sakha people. I told her she was an answer to my prayers, and I promised to pray regularly for her.

The whole year I was gone, I prayed for Luba's growth. When I returned, I discovered the Lord had allowed her to go through many trials. I cringed while she told me about the facial surgery she had endured—without anesthesia! The surgeons told her later that she was one of their bravest patients ever. She had depended on the Lord for strength, she told them.

Also during our absence, Luba's father died. She sang Christian songs and witnessed to him as she cared for him in his last days. After the funeral, she found a note in the Bible she had given him. It said, "With all my heart and body, I have prayed sincerely in the name of the Lord God. I believe indeed that the Lord God is alive. The Lord God is Truth."

Luba demonstrated a quiet and gentle spirit to her unbelieving husband and children. A couple of years later, they committed themselves to the Lord and were baptized in the lake near our house. Luba's son and daughter, both musicians, enjoy ministering in church and hope to make music their profession.

Because she was one of the few women whose entire family had come to the Lord, Luba was invited to a nearby town to speak to the church ladies on how to be a witness to an unsaved husband. It was clear that Luba was not only gifted in singing, but in evangelism as well.

Her growing credibility is a joy to see.

For several years, Luba has led a Sakha singing group at our church. This has made Sakha people feel more comfortable about using their heart language in worship and prayer. I attended their song rehearsals and watched as Luba developed extraordinary leadership skills. Now she has begun recording a CD called *Lubov* ("Love"), singing Sakha songs about love.

Luba is God's gift to the Sakha church. She is the only Sakha Christian I know who can sing *toyuk*, the highly-ornamented and improvisatory traditional genre that is so valued by the Sakha people. This genre is a powerful means of communication with rural Sakha people, especially the elderly, who consider it their "heart music." Luba is especially excited about a sub-genre of toyuk called *kepseen*, an improvised style that allows her to say what is on her heart—through song. And that heart nearly bursts with the joyful gospel of Jesus Christ.

Most churches in this Siberian republic are less than ten years old, and less than five hundred Sakha evangelical believers attend. It may be some time before urban bi-ethnic (Russian-Sakha) churches are able to accept traditional Sakha song styles as a part of their worship services. In rural settings, however, acceptance is growing. A Christian version of *ohuokai*, a traditional Sakha round dance, is now performed at the yearly Sakha Christian conference. It's an encouraging development that shows a desire for expressing faith through God-given cultural forms.

My plea for a Sahka music friend was abundantly answered. Luba proved to be an ethnomusicologist's dream for a partner in ministry. In addition, she is an expert on Sahka culture and an encouraging friend. With Love at work through Luba and others, we fully expect tolerance and ambivalence toward Sakha song styles will one day yield to open-hearted acceptance.

Epilogue

In 2005, Luba accompanied a group of Sakha musicians to Beijing, China, where they won a prize at the international festival of music "Pearls of the East." They have subsequently received invitations to perform at a summer 2006 festival in Tunis and at the 2008 Olympics in Beijing.

Chapter 11

Siberia

A New Song and a New Mom
by Dave and Kay Henry

Afanasi yearned to write an *ohuokai,* a round dance song. In the past, his father had often written ones that praised nature, but Afanasi wanted to praise his Creator God. A Yakut* from Siberia, he had acknowledged Christ as his Lord three years before. Consequently, he had developed two strong desires: to write an ohuokai and to see his relatives come to know Jesus Christ as their Savior too.

During the winter months, Afanasi traveled to his birthplace near Suntar to witness to those relatives. He was especially burdened for an elderly uncle who was ill. The uncle and other relatives gladly received him and listened to his testimony, but no one repented of their sins. Afanasi also traveled many miles to the capital, Yakutsk, to witness to his mother. And he continued to pray. He later invited her to a Christian conference and was excited when she agreed to accompany him.

Yakut people from all over the Republic of Yakutia gathered in Oktyomtsi in March 2004 for the sixth annual Yakut Christian Conference. "You Are the Light of the World," proclaimed the conference banner in Yakut, quoting Matthew 5:14. Guests attended meetings in the village community center and were housed and fed by the thirty members of Oktyomtsi Evangelical Christian Church. They had expected 100–120 to come, but 180 showed up!

That year the conference featured their Yakut heritage and culture. More than twenty people came dressed in colorful, national dress, including Afanasi's mother.

Yakut people joyfully participated in the opening national round dance—a Christian ohuokai from the Yakut hymnal. Afanasi also joined in, not forgetting his desire to write his own composition.

The leader of the ohuokai would sing one line, and the rest of the people would repeat it—a call-and-response. Where possible, participants formed a large circle, linking arms as they gracefully and joyfully moved in harmony. Indeed, the Yakut church was becoming more Yakutian.

The night before the conference ended, Afanasi finally was able to write an ohuokai and sang it on the last day. His mother joined in. His song praised God as the Creator and told about the blessing of God's good news coming to the land of the Yakut people. Two other people also wrote and led new ohuokai songs.

Afanasi's mother had planned to attend the conference only one day, but ended up staying all three. On the last day, seven Yakut people prayed to receive the Lord as their Savior—and the first in line was Afanasi's mother.

Yakut people continue to lead in their churches, writing more original songs and also serving as missionaries to their own people. Repenting, finding Christ, burdened for the salvation of others, they praise and worship the Creator—through ohuokai songs—in spirit and in truth.

Epilogue

Afanasi has been faithfully serving as a missionary in his hometown near Suntar since May 2005. There are now six adult believers and twelve to fifteen children who regularly attend services twice a week. Afanasi's mother is also growing spiritually. She attends a weekly Bible study in the Yakut language in the city of Yakutsk.

---

*An alternate name for Yakut is Sakha.

This article is adapted from "On the Third Day, Afanasi Had a New Mother," in *InterACTION,* summer 2004, a publication of InterAct Ministries.

Chapter 12

Colombia

The Night of the Tiger
by Bruce Olson

I was lying in my hammock after the morning hunt. The women were cooking, and the acrid smoke of the fires, mixed with the smell of roasting monkey, made me drowsy. Soon it would be time to eat. I was hungry.

I heard a commotion in the other end of the home and lifted myself up on my elbow to see what was happening. A little knot of men and women had gathered around Abacuriana, a young, slender man. I caught a few of his words.

"Tiger . . . I couldn't move. . . . " He was talking excitedly.

Two men in hammocks near me got up and started toward the cluster of people. "Hey, Chanti." I called to one of them. "What's going on?"

He came over to my hammock. He seemed nervous.

"Didn't you hear?" he asked hoarsely. "The tiger spoke."

"What tiger?" I said, confused. "Spoke what? What are you talking about?"

"The tiger spoke! He spoke!"

I shook my head. "Chanti, tigers don't speak. And if they did, who would care what they said?"

"Oh," he said, "when the tiger speaks we are in big trouble. Big, big trouble."

By this time, his eyes were rolling. "Okay, thanks," I said, and let him go.

The whole house was in an uproar. All work stopped. Those who couldn't get close to Abacuriana stood on the perimeter of the crowd and talked, or walked swiftly to the door and stared outside.

I got out of my hammock. The chief was standing at one of the doors. I drew him aside.

"I want to talk to you," I said. "What does it mean that the tiger spoke?"

"It means we're in for big trouble," he said.

"But what kind of trouble? What could a tiger say that would be dangerous?"

"I'm going into the jungle to talk to the tiger. He'll tell me."

"But chief," I said, "tigers don't talk. This is nonsense."

He gave me a quick, hard glance. "Look," he said, "you don't know anything about the jungle. You don't know how to hunt; you don't know what to eat. You can't keep up on the trail. What makes you think you know anything about tigers?"

There wasn't much I could say. I looked at him in nervous astonishment, while he stared coldly into the jungle. Then, with monumental effort, he squared his shoulders and walked out of the house. I watched him cross the clearing and disappear, alone, into the trees. I turned. Everyone in the home was looking at the area where he had disappeared.

He was gone until late afternoon. Everyone waited for him to return. No one worked. A few men tried to carve arrows, but they would stop often and stare into space. There was very little talking. People walked restlessly around the house, and their restlessness was transferred to me. I couldn't sit still. What was going on? I had never seen anything like this. The house seemed to be pressed down by a huge, invisible hand.

When the chief came back, people immediately huddled around him. He waited to speak until everyone had gathered. His face was tired and drawn. He seemed to have aged ten years.

"The tiger says that the spirits will come out of the rocks tonight. They will attack this home. Lives will be snuffed out. Languages will cease. There will be death."

In profound silence, the chief walked off and got in his hammock. People wandered off by themselves.

What on earth is going on? I wondered. *Where did all this fear come from? What does it mean, that the tiger speaks and spirits come out of the rocks?*

It was obvious that something really terrifying was happening. These people were not normally superstitious, and I had never, never seen them really frightened before. They routinely faced poisonous snakes and dangerous animals, and never showed a trace of fear. If they were afraid now, there must be something worth being afraid of. But what was it? How could they fight it?

I found Bobby outside the home, staring off into the distance. He glanced over at me when I came up.

"Bruchko, can Jesus be taken out of my mouth?" he asked, a tense edge of fear in his voice.

"Bobby, what is this all about? What does it mean that the tiger speaks? What does it mean that the spirits will come out of the rocks?"

"The spirits come out of the rocks," he said. "They try to kill. Sometimes only one dies. Sometimes many die. In Ocbabuda two months ago seven died."

"How do they die?" I asked. "What kills them?"

"The spirits kill them, Bruchko," he said. "They die in their hammocks because the evil spirits tear their language away from them."

"Bobby, does someone always die?"

"Always," he said.

The air seemed thick. What did this mean? Why did I feel under so much pressure?

"Can Jesus be taken out of my mouth?" Bobby asked again, looking out into the jungle.

I didn't know how to answer him. I had never before dealt with demon powers. I felt frightened, too.

"Can the devil kill me now that I walk in Jesus' path?" he continued. "Bruchko, what am I to do?"

"I don't know, Bobby. You'll have to talk to Jesus yourself. He is the only one who has the answer to your questions. He will speak to you in your heart."

He hesitated, then walked off into the jungle. I immediately felt regret. Why hadn't I given him some advice? What kind of spiritual father was I?

But I didn't have any advice to give.

I went for a long walk into the jungle. I was not only frightened but confused. "Tigers can't talk," I told God. "What is happening here?"

When I got back to the home it was nearly dark. As soon as I entered the clearing I heard strange, high wailings and incantations. The house was swaying back and forth, as if possessed by the devil himself. The incantations were jumbled. They went up and down, gathering force, then dropping. The air seemed electric. I was almost afraid to enter.

Inside the fires cast an eerie red glow. I saw that the house indeed was swaying. All the men, high up in their hammocks, were swinging and chanting to ward off the devil. The women were on the floor, clapping large rocks together. Their eyes—like the eyes of the men—were tightly closed.

Where was Bobby? Was he in this place? Suddenly I was afraid for him. He was the only Motilone who had begun to walk Jesus' trail. Had he given in to this fear and superstition?

Then I saw his hammock. He was in it, swinging. I almost turned back and into the jungle. But something restrained me. He was my brother.

I grasped one of the poles that supported the house and began to shinny up toward Bobby's hammock, which was almost twenty feet above the floor. The bamboo bent under my weight, and I wondered if it would hold me. But Bobby's welfare was the most important thing in the world to me just then. Hand over hand, I pulled myself up. When I got high enough, I looked into Bobby's hammock. His eyes were open. He had a big smile on his face. The song he was singing was different:

> "Jesus is in my mouth;
> I have a new speech.
> Jesus is in my mouth;
> no one can take Him from me.
> I speak Jesus' words.
> I walk in Jesus' steps.
> I am Jesus' boy;
> He had filled my stomach, and I am no longer hungry."

As I clung to the palm tree pole, Bobby looked straight at me. He was safe. He knew Jesus. He was doing the thing I should have had the vision to suggest. He was keeping the evil spirits away by singing a song of Jesus.

I joined him in the song. All that night we sang. When dawn came, no one had died. It was the first time in anyone's memory that the spirits had walked and no one had died.

No one commented on Bobby's song, yet I could sense that the other Motilones had a new interest in him and in his relationship to Jesus. It wasn't particularly outward; that wasn't the Motilone way. But the evidence was clear.

And Bobby began to change. In the months that followed his commitment to Jesus, he became less proud. When he visited other homes, he accepted food immediately instead of forcing himself to go without it to demonstrate his strength. That stubbornness had not made him very popular among the other men, though they respected him for it. Now they noticed his new attitude and wondered what caused it.

I was eager for Bobby to tell them. He could do it more effectively than I, I was sure. I tried to encourage him to share his experiences, and was upset when he didn't. Was it because he didn't care enough about the other Motilones? I couldn't be sure.

But I was trying to squeeze him into "the mold" and didn't realize it. News has no real significance to the Motilones until it's given in a formal ceremony. In my excitement over Bobby's spiritual experience, I wanted him to do things the way they would have been done in North America. I wanted him to call a meeting and tell about Jesus, or corner his friends and explain what Jesus now meant to him. But thank God he waited until he could do it the Motilone way.

Word spread that there was to be another Festival of the Arrows. There was excitement in the home. The Festival was the only time all the Motilones gathered together.

Pacts would be formed. Arrows would be exchanged, and the men forming the pact would have a singing contest. They would climb into their hammocks and sing as long as they could, relating legends, stories, and news, or recent events. Often their songs would last twelve hours, without interruption for food, water, or rest.

People streamed into the home. There was lots of noise and food. Old friends greeted each other, and swapped stories. People were looking at Bobby in a new light. Word had spread about the night the spirits had walked and no one had died. He was looked on with respect, and some curiosity. He had married, and was accepted as a man.

An older chief named Adjibacbayra took a special interest in Bobby. His reserved air made him appear dignified. However, he had a lot of curiosity, and on the first day of the Festival, challenged Bobby to a song. Bobby was pleased, and immediately accepted.

They both climbed into a single hammock twenty feet off the ground, and began to swing back and forth. Bobby sang first, and Adjibacbayra imitated him, following line for line. Other men also had challenged each other to songs, and were singing.

Bobby's song was about the way the Motilones had been deceived and had lost God's trail. He told how they had once known God, but had been greedy and had followed a false prophet. Then he began to sing about Jesus. As he did so, the other men who were singing stopped. Everyone became quiet in order to listen.

"Jesus Christ was incarnated into man," Bobby sang. "He has walked our trails. He is God yet we can know him."

The home was deathly still, except for Bobby's wailing song and Adjibacbayra's repetition. People were straining their ears to hear.

Inside me, however, a spiritual battle was raging. I found myself hating the song. It seemed so heathen. The music, chanted in a strange minor key, sounded like witch music. It seemed to degrade the gospel. Yet when I looked at the people around me, and up at the chief swinging in his hammock, I could see that they were listening as though their lives depended on it. Bobby was giving them spiritual truth through the song.

Still I wanted to do it *my* way—until I heard Bobby sing about Jesus giving him a new language.

"Can't you see the reality that he is giving to them?" God seemed to ask me.

"But Lord," I replied, "why am I so repulsed by it?"

Then I saw that it was because I was sinful. I could love the Motilone way of life, but when it came to spiritual matters I thought I had the only way. But my way wasn't necessarily God's way. God was saying, "I too love the Motilone way of life. I made it. And I'm going to tell them about my Son in *my* way."

I relaxed, able at last to find real joy in Bobby's song. It continued for eight hours, ten hours. Attention didn't slacken. It got dark inside the house. Fires were built. Finally, after fourteen hours, they quit singing and climbed wearily down from their hammock.

Adjibacbayra looked at Bobby. "You've communicated a true news item," he said. "I too want to suspend myself in Jesus. I want to pull his blood over my deception."

That night a spiritual revolution swept over the people. No one rejected the news about Jesus. Everyone wanted him to take them over the horizon. There was tremendous jubilation. Sometimes it was quiet and people would talk to each other in little groups. At other times, the joy would break into spontaneous singing. It went late into the night.

God had spoken. He had spoken in the Motilone language, and through the Motilone culture. He had not even had to use me.

"The Night of the Tiger" is a true story from the book *Bruchko* by Bruce Olson. Charisma House 1973, 1995, pages 140–146. The book was originally titled *For This Cross I'll Kill You.* Used by permission.

Chapter 13

Côte d'Ivoire and Liberia

"Teach Us the Songs of Heaven!"
An African Evangelist
Encourages Indigenous Hymnody*
by James R. Krabill

William Wadé Harris, the Prophet-Evangelist and "Ethnohymnologist"

When late in 1913 Prophet William Wadé Harris left his native Liberia to begin his now well-known evangelistic campaign through southern Ivory Coast, he found himself confronted with a population having had little, if any, previous exposure to Christianity. French Catholic missionaries had for almost twenty years been working tirelessly at establishing a credible and lasting presence in the area, but had met with limited success. And the only Protestant presence was found in small and scattered groups of African English-speaking clerks from Sierra Leone, the Gold Coast, Liberia, and The Gambia, who had come to Ivory Coast, not as missionaries, but as agents of British trading companies doing business with coastal peoples.

The prophet's preaching, fetish-burning, and baptizing ministry lasted a mere eighteen months until his expulsion from the colony in January 1915. The impact of that brief ministry, however, was most remarkable indeed, resulting in:

- an estimated 100,000–200,000 persons turning from traditional religious beliefs and practices toward a new reality structured around certain rudimentary tenets of the Christian faith as prescribed by Prophet Harris;
- worship of the "one, true God";
- weekly gathering on the seventh day for preaching, prayer, and singing;
- initial exposure to God's law in the Ten Commandments and to the Lord's Prayer;
- and the choosing of new "religious specialists" (preachers and twelve apostles) responsible in each village for watching over the general well-being of the church.

In general, Prophet Harris was a man on the move, never lingering long in any one location. In some instances, villagers would travel long distances to see the prophet, receive baptism from his hand, then return home all in the same day, never to see him again.

One of the questions frequently asked of Harris by new converts during those brief encounters concerned the type of music they were expected to sing once they arrived back home in their villages. "Teach us the songs of heaven," they pleaded with the prophet, "so we can truly bring glory to God."

It is important to understand Harris' background in order to appreciate his response to the thousands of new believers who crowded around him, clinging almost desperately to every word of counsel he could give them. Born of a Methodist mother, probably around 1860, William Wadé Harris had spent over thirty-five years—nearly all of his pre-prophetic adult life (1873–1910)—attending and actively serving the "civilized" Methodist and Episcopal churches of eastern Liberia. Quite understandably, the Western hymn traditions that filled the liturgies of these churches had come to be the sacred music dearly loved and cherished by Harris as well. When asked in 1978 whether Harris had any favorite hymns, the prophet's grandchildren recalled without hesitation, "Lo, He Comes with Clouds Descending" (his favorite hymn, which he sang repeatedly),

"Guide Me, O Thou Great Jehovah," "Jesus, Lover of My Soul," "How Firm a Foundation, Ye Saints of the Lord," and "What a Friend We Have in Jesus."

Yet faced with the crowd seeking his advice on this most important matter, the prophet refused easy answers. "I have never been to heaven," he wisely told them, "so I cannot tell you what kind of music is sung in God's royal village. But know this," he continued, "that God has no personal favorite songs. He hears all that we say in whatever language. It is sufficient for us to compose hymns of praise to him with our own music and in our own language for him to understand."

When asked further how exactly they were to proceed in composing these new "songs of God," the prophet told the people to begin by using the music and dance forms with which they were already acquainted. For the Dida people—one of the first and largest ethnic groups to feel the impact of the prophet's ministry—this represented a remarkable repertoire of at least thirty distinct classifications of traditional musical genres, ranging from love ballads and funeral dirges to songs composed for hunting, rice planting, and rendering homage to wealthy community leaders.

Not all musical genres, however, were suitable, according to the prophet, for use in praising God. The following story from late 1913 describes how Harris helped the Dida people in the coastal village of Lauzoua to identify what kind of traditional music might best be used in hymn composition.

> The prophet requested a calabash [rhythmical gourd instrument] from one of the women traveling with him and handed it to Dogbontcho, a well-known local female musician-composer. Dogbontcho in turn began singing for Harris a *zlanje* tune [a classification of traditional love songs among the Dida]. When she had finished, Harris said, "That song does not honor God! Sing another kind!"
>
> This time Dogbontcho chose a *dogblo* tune [traditional praise song of political or religious patronage]:

He who does not worship God will worship fetishes instead;
But the day that God tells him,
"Follow me and abandon your fetishes,"
That day he will have to do what God commands him.

The entire population of Lauzoua soon broke out in song joining in behind their lead singer. The prophet himself, carried away by the rhythm of the music, climbed out of his canoe and began dancing. And then a miracle happened as the paralytic Dogbontcho herself abandoned her cane and began dancing with the prophet, accompanied by the entire population of Lauzoua now overcome with joy.

Following this miracle, the prophet counseled the people of Lauzoua to refrain henceforth from using their dogblo music for profane purposes, but to dedicate it instead to God, transforming it bit by bit and in such a way that it might bring glory to God. And this is how the traditional dogblo music of the Dida of Lauzoua and Yocoboué became the sacred music of the church that took shape following the prophet's coming to these parts.**

Setting the New Faith to Music

Encouraged by these words of counsel and armed with the confidence that they were themselves capable of producing music acceptable to God, Dida composers set to work, expressing with great enthusiasm their new-found faith:

We, too, we have at last found our Father.
We did not know that we were going to find our Father.
But we have found our Father;
Our Father is the King of Glory.

One group of old men from the Dida village of Makey reported to me in 1984 that Harris, in his Lauzoua statement, had given two very specific guidelines for the composition of hymns: 1) that traditional praise songs (literally, songs that "hurl forth" or "shout out the name of someone") should be employed in the creation of new songs, intended now to bring praise to God; and 2) that much use should be made of "forgiveness language" —language ordinarily employed by an individual who "wishes to reestablish with some other person a relationship that has been broken or in some significant way greatly marred." It is remarkable how many of the earliest Harrist hymns do, in fact, seem to express one or another aspect of these two themes of praise and forgiveness.

The dogblo style dates back to the earliest years of the Harrist movement. It was followed by the *yedje* style, originating from the Avikam people who live along the coast, and becoming a part of the Dida Harrist corpus from the 1930s onward. These were later supplemented by the *ŋodilo, ébrié,* and *nouveautés* music. Ɖodilo, meaning "young men's songs," have been written from the 1920s onwards to counteract and complement what was otherwise a musical world dominated by women. Ébrié hymns are those brought to Dida territory following the 1949 visit of John Ahui, the then-recognized spiritual head of the Harrist Church in the Ivory Coast. Nouveautés (the newest, latest hymns) date from about 1965 onward.

In the years that followed, Harrist composers found and developed additional music styles as they learned to read the Scriptures and grew in Christian understanding. They developed a justifiable pride in this achievement: one Dida hymn dating from the 1920s defends their practice from the criticism of Protestant missionaries and catechists ("the Bible people"):

> We have Your Name, yes indeed!
> Yet the Bible people tell us
> That with the work we are doing here,
> We cannot come near to the Lord.
> Why can't we come near to the Father? . . .
>
> Let us take our own wisdom and pray to the Lord . . .
>
> Each village has its own language;
> Take this then to pray to the Father!

In the years that followed the prophet's swift passage through southern Ivory Coast, Dida Harrist composers produced an amazing number of hymns. My work with Dida leadership in collecting and transcribing Harrist hymns brought to light over five hundred hymn texts spanning the 75-year period from 1913 to 1988. Since my departure from Ivory Coast in 1996, scores of new compositions have been added to the list.

A Model for Today

Studies in recent years made by missionary anthropologists and Christian ethnomusicologists have increasingly insisted upon the following affirmations:

1) That "although God exists totally outside of culture, while humans exist totally within culture, God chooses the cultural milieu in which humans are immersed as the arena for his interaction with people." (Charles Kraft in Martin Wroe, "Ancient and Modern: Church Music and the Culture Gap," *The Third Way* (August 1985), p. 22.)

2) That Western culture with its particular musical traditions has been in the past and can be today one such arena for God's interaction with people. Should, however, Western culture, Western languages, and Western music come to be perceived as the only or even preferred arena for God's activity, then we are faced with a misconception that is "not only culturally stultifying but also theological heresy" (Albert W. D. Friesen in his unpublished thesis "A Methodology in the Development of Indigenous Hymnody," 1981:ii-iii.)

3) That God can inspire and speak through *every* culture, *every* language, and *every* music system, regardless of whether persons outside of that culture have an aesthetic response to it. To deny this is to deny the universality of God. (Cf. Vida Chenoweth, "Spare Them Western Music!" *Evangelical Missions Quarterly* 20 (1) January (1984), p. 30.)

The Prophet Harris never claimed to be a theologian, much less a cultural anthropologist or an ethnomusicologist. But today's ethnohymnologists, trained as they are in these disciplines, could do worse if ever they were to choose him as their patron saint. "God has no personal, favorite songs," Harris told the Dida people at Lauzoua. "He hears all that we say in whatever language; it is sufficient for us to praise him in our own language for him to understand."

*This article is based upon several sections from my published dissertation, "The Hymnody of the Harrist Church Among the Dida of South-central Ivory Coast (1913–1949): An Historico-Religious Study" [Studies in the Intercultural History of Christianity, Vol. 74] Frankfurt am Main: Peter Lang GmbH, 1995, 603 pp. An earlier article covering much of the same material was published under the title, "William Wadé Harris (1860-1929): African Evangelist and 'Ethnohymnologist,'" *Mission Focus* 18 (4) December (1990), pp. 56–59.

**For a fuller account of Harris' advice to the Dida people of Lauzoua, see my article, "Dida Harrist Hymnody (1913–1990)" in *Journal of Religion in Africa* XX (2) June (1990), pp. 119–120. A more recent rendition of the story is available in Chapter 7 ("Gospel Meets Culture") of my book, *Is It Insensitive to Share Your Faith?* Intercourse, PA: Good Books, 2005, pp. 88–102.

Movement 1:
Workshop as Musical
Catalyst

Chapter 14

Côte d'Ivoire

Abraham Goes Senufo:
Communicating the Scriptures through Song
by Roberta R. King

As we pulled into the northern town of Ferkessédougou, Côte d'Ivoire, I thought, *What a providential time for a New Song Workshop designed to set the life of Abraham to song!* The community was preparing for *Tabaski,* a celebration of the life of Abraham, with emphasis on God's requiring him to sacrifice his son, Ishmael, per their tradition. Known as the "Big Feast," sheep and goats would be slaughtered and then feasted upon at the end of a formal worship ritual.

Dusty, desert-like Ferkessédougou (known as Ferké) is a communication crossroads among three diverse West African nations: Côte d'Ivoire, Burkina Faso, and Mali. In its town square, huge semi-trucks, garishly painted in shockingly bright colors, were either crammed with live cattle or loaded sky-high with the limited manufactured goods that manage to make it to this desolate region. Besides this, the main plaza teemed with growing numbers of sheep and goats, roaming freely around the lone, stark obelisk that serves as a war memorial. Although the physical setting is stark, Ferké is a place I have come to love.

Along one side of the town square lies the mission compound where the ten-day New Song Workshop took place from February 11–20, 2002.

Senufo Believers Grab Hold of the Blessing

Forty believers from Côte d'Ivoire and Mali attended my classes, representing four Senufo language groups: Nyarafolo,* Shenara, Minyanka, and Djimini. I looked at them and asked God for the wisdom to share about his faithfulness and desire to bless them through the story of Abraham. They came from both towns and villages, some able to read, others dependent on oral communication. Being oral learners, their primary means of receiving information is through songs and stories. They came longing to learn the Scriptures—in a way that would be meaningful and enjoyable to them. Their eagerness to worship God and grow in him resulted in the most successful workshop to date.

The workshop—setting the life of Abraham as recorded in Genesis 12–22 to song—did not function separately from local churches and missions. Rather, it enhanced translation and church planting projects among the Senufo peoples. This included setting newly translated passages to song and simultaneously developing an oral translation of the Scriptures.

The overall mission strategy is to present translated Scriptures chronologically, building a growing foundation for understanding who Jesus Christ is. Several mission and church groups** participated in the workshop by sending church leaders, translation teams, or singers. The songs produced will be used in a cassette ministry, with hopes they will be sung regularly in churches and eventually get radio airplay.

The workshop approach allows national believers to set longer passages of Scripture to song in their own language and musical styles. It is essential that singers first internalize the story well. Then they must allow the teachings about God to inspire them in transforming the Scripture passage into their own authentic and distinctive song forms. This method, developed over the last thirteen years, has proved effective. (see King 1999, 101–125).

Each day we began with a plenary session that included studies on music in the Bible, worship, and prayer. Then, dividing into three teams, we worked with the designated text, averaging one to two chapters of Genesis per day. Three of the language groups had enough participants to form a distinct *New Song Fellowship*. The fourth language group had only one representative, a Shenara-speaking pastor. He chose to move among the teams, often helping by playing the *balafon* (xylophone) after songs had been composed.

Each team read and discussed the newly translated Scriptures on Abraham's life in their vernacular language—an essential to creating indigenous songs since melodic and rhythmic contours of the song are intimately wed to patterns in the language. Working in vernacular languages also allowed women, who often speak only their mother-tongue, to participate freely.

The overarching workshop goal was to communicate the life of Abraham through indigenous song creation. However, teaching and learning the Scriptures remained the focal point. Indeed, many heard the story for the first time in their own language and were amazed at God's faithfulness to Abraham. For example, when Abram and Sarai tried to take things into their own hands, such as having a child through Hagar, God remained faithful to His promise to bless Abraham and his family. (Senufo customs and cultural practices share so many similarities with the biblical text that workshop participants wondered whose culture came first, theirs or the Israelites'.)

Most amazing to them was the story of God demanding the sacrifice of Isaac. (The religious book many people in this area follow never mentions a specific name in reference to the sacrifice of Abraham's son. Yet, traditionally in this area, they speak of the sacrifice of Ishmael, not Isaac, as portrayed in Genesis 22.) They weren't sure they wanted to sing about this part of Abraham's life, afraid that their families would reject a God who demanded human sacrifice. Yet, in struggling through the passage, they reasoned this was God's Word and they must be faithful to tell the whole story. They later came to realize the impact and wonder of God faithfully providing the required sacrifice and its symbolic significance for the future coming of Jesus Christ. God was also preparing their hearts to sing about him.

And what about the songs? Each day, after interacting with Scripture, both in their small teams and then together, they composed songs in their own languages. Amazingly, songs began to emerge; at first slowly and tentatively. As they were sung for the first time, they often improved as the group contributed additional musical ideas. Later, songs exploded, almost like popcorn.

As we "harvested" songs each day in the combined group, people spontaneously responded to ones that spoke on a deep level and in authentic Senufo musical styles; they rose up and danced with joyful abandon. Such Christian fellowship was an intoxicating and edifying experience for both insiders and outsiders.

In six days, the Lord gave a total of forty-seven new songs telling "redemption history" through Abraham's story. And in one-and-a-half days, forty-two songs were recorded, and four CDs burned: two CDs for Nyarafolo (twenty-four songs), while the Djimini and Minyanka composed enough songs for one CD each. The singers were then able to take the CDs home to use as masters for making audiocassettes to help teach Scripture in their communities and churches.

Dynamics of a Successful Workshop

The outpouring of creativity in a successful New Song Workshop, such as we experienced in Ferké, springs from multiple dynamics. Below are five that especially contribute to the mission task of bringing all nations to worship before him (Psalm 86:9).

1. Applying Scripture to Everyday Life

Presenting and teaching Scripture to a people for the first time in their own language is a privilege and an awe-inspiring task. The ultimate goal is to help a language group learn how God can be a real part of their everyday life as they practice biblical faith (Gilliland, 227). For example, a special moment in the workshop came when the believers discovered that Abraham had such great faith and allegiance to God that he would turn down the spoils of war offered him. Indeed, Abraham had sworn to God that he would accept nothing belonging to the king of Sodom, and that is just what he told the king (Genesis 14:22–24).

Abraham's keeping his oath spoke profoundly to people who rarely see promises kept. In addition, most people barely make more than twenty-five cents a day in income and would find it difficult to turn down an offer of riches. Abraham's choice painted an intimate relationship with the God who comes close and is a part of our daily lives—a great contrast to their concept of a distant and angry god. Such an approach to applied ethnomusicology creates opportunities for sacred moments when the truth of the Word can be planted deeply within people's thinking and lifestyles.

2. The Ethnomusicologist as Midwife

In leading such a workshop, my role is that of a musical midwife. I patiently wait for the music to come from the people, gently and prayerfully coaxing songs out of them. Colleagues have asked, "How do you make that happen? We live with these people all year long and never see them compose songs like these."

What is going on here? Two things. First, we come not just as musicians who happen to be Christians, wanting to play a part in the mission task—even though that can be a valid entry point. Rather, we come as ministers of the gospel, and *music* simply provides a platform for communicating that good news on a deep level in cultural contexts.

Second, relating as musicians to musicians adds to the dynamics of the workshop. When we as musicians have taken time to learn the musical culture, we receive great credibility and influence, and the right to help "birth" new songs. Because I spent significant time researching Senufo music and Christian songs for my PhD studies (King 1989), people recognize how much I value their music and way of life. My affirmation of their culture and music releases them to sing freely in worship to Almighty God.

At the end of our workshop a missionary colleague acknowledged, "The magic was here again. Well, really we know it was the Holy Spirit." In essence, such a ministry is dependent on the credibility and spirituality of the ethnomusicologist as he or she interacts with the people.

3. Musical Innovation Is a Process

The development of heart-level songs that inspire genuine worship can take years. In previous years, we developed a Senufo song form with a high text load (many words in the song text). This allows Senufo believers to "preach" via their songs. Each time I return to the area, I am pleased to see how this song form has grown in cultural authenticity and musical complexity.

Parallel to musical growth, it appears that spiritual maturity liberates people to respond more authentically in their singing style as time goes on. Discerning what is helpful to their Christian worship increases the more they understand that God accepts them as they are and that they have permission to draw from their cultural heritage.

The Nyarafolo, for example, suddenly felt they no longer had to imitate the neighboring Cebaara Christian worship style that incorporates the *balafon* (a 19-key, wood-frame xylophone). As the Nyarafolos began to sing about the sacrifice of Isaac (Genesis 22), they realized its import and wanted to add more weight to the impact of the song. They decided to leave out Cebaara balafons and use only their percussion instruments. They claimed this provided a truly indigenous sound and an authentic rhythm that fit the message of their song. I had falsely assumed that the balafon was part of the Nyarafolos' repertoire of instruments. Such a sophisticated development came only after many years of working together toward worship songs that would speak meaningfully to them.

4. Meeting Felt Needs and Agendas

If at all possible, we respond to the felt needs of the musicians. Each group in this workshop was at a different place in the continuum toward developing indigenous, culturally-appropriate songs. The Minyanka group, for example, had come with a pressing issue. Drums were in use in their church, but the leadership had not yet allowed the balafon. Therefore, the Minyanka men wanted to know if they could worship God with their balafon.

We discussed that question when the Nyarafolo women needed to go to market on Thursday to purchase food, making good use of that supposedly lost time. I taught the men, the ones who traditionally play the musical instruments, about the use of instruments in the Scriptures. They responded well and as a result, we soon found they were able to participate more freely and fruitfully in composing new songs. The song harvest continued to increase.

5. Advantages of Multiple-Language Workshops

In past workshops, I have preferred to work with only one language group at a time. Yet, in this workshop with four languages represented, the synergy heightened both song-making and Christian fellowship. The Nyarafolo group, already accustomed to such a workshop, could both develop their new set of songs and also model for the other groups how they could compose their own songs.

In addition, everyone had an opportunity to fellowship together in a region where Christians are few. One group was experiencing persecution in their village. They were encouraged and strengthened to hear how God was working among other Senufo believers. Thus, learning to relate to the family of God added to the important role of building positive relationships, ones that contribute to the spiritual growth of the church. The newly-formed friendships also contributed to their growing understanding that God wants to bless all peoples, just as he had blessed Abraham's family.

Conclusion

The Abrahamic blessing continues among the Senufo. Though the workshop ended, the Scripture-in-song lessons have not. Each language group took with them the ability to continue composing songs based on scriptural passages in their mother tongue. As Senufo believers return to their churches, towns, and villages, they are committed to singing the new songs. They will use them in worship, evangelism, and various life events, such as funerals. They are even becoming missionaries to one another. The lone Shenara-speaking pastor has invited the Nyarafolo believers to hold a New Song Workshop for his people in Mali.

As we drove out of dusty Ferké, the Tabaski celebration had just concluded. Several thousand people, dressed up for the occasion in their long, brightly colored robes, were milling around the open square. A perfectly white ram, without a single spot, had just been ritually slaughtered. Yet, as the people disbursed, they seemed oblivious to the slain animal. I wondered what they really understood about the God of Abraham. I prayed that the new songs about Abraham and the faithfulness of God would make a difference in extending his blessings to all peoples in this region of Africa.

*The Nyarafolo people with whom I have worked intermittently since 1990 are young believers who sincerely seek to worship the true and living God. They long to bring their families to freedom in Christ so they will also share in the blessing that was foretold to Abraham, the man of faith (Galatians 3:9).

**The groups included CB International, The International Mission Board (Southern Baptist), the Baptist churches in Côte d'Ivoire, and the Assemblies of God of Ferkessédougou.

References cited

Gilliland, Dean. "Contextualization" in *Evangelical Dictionary of 2000 World Mission*, A. Scott Moreau, Harold Netland, and Charles Van Engen, Eds. Pp. 225–228. Grand Rapids, MI: Baker Books.

King, Roberta A. *Time to Sing: A Manual for the African Church*. Nairobi, 1999. Kenya: Evangel Publishing House.

_____. 1989. *Pathways in Christian Music Communication: the Case of the Senufo of Côte d'Ivoire*. Pasadena, CA: Fuller Theological Seminary PhD. Dissertation (available through University Microfilms).

This article is an adaptation of its first edition published in *EthnoDoxology*, 1:2, (2002).

Chapter 15

Ghana

User-Friendly Hymns for the Achoday
by Paul Neeley

"How did Jesus walk on the water?"

"What is this heavenly town of Jerusalem like?"

"How did these Bible stories get turned into our kind of songs?"

Achoday* people ask us questions such as these when they hear the good news presented on cassette—in their heart language and heart music. For many of them, this is the first time they have ever heard Scripture.

The fifteen thousand Achoday people of eastern Ghana, Africa, practice a traditional religion based, in part, around a famous and powerful shrine and its priesthood. The women's cult (*Oku–Oku*), built around the python snake, also thrives. Although churches and schools have been in the area more than fifty years, the impact of Christianity and education is still insignificant—about 3 percent of the people attend church on a semi-regular basis. A mother-tongue literacy program has been ongoing for more than ten years.

In January 1994, a series of Scripture Use workshops in the Volta region of Ghana helped five language groups, including the Achoday. We recorded an hour-long cassette of Bible readings and associated Scripture songs, composed, for the most part, in Achoday musical styles.

When we played the tape at a central meeting place in the village, about a dozen shrine priests listened with great interest and asked questions raised by the Scripture readings. "What did the dove at Jesus' baptism symbolize?" "Where is the Jordan River?"

"It is very good to hear our language and music on cassette," they concluded. "If you buy us a drink, we can dance to the songs in the afternoon!"

Shrine priests have strong taboos against anything to do with church and literacy in any language. So they will probably never *read* any Scripture portion. Yet a number of them purchased their own cassettes and played them for their peers. Give it to them in a user-friendly form—with their own singing and drumming—and they are ready to listen and discuss.

Co-wives stay up late in the night to hear the cassette. This stimulates new interest in Bible stories and gives rise to questions such as, "Are these stories true?" "Where did these stories take place?" "Where is Jesus now?"

At other villages, as soon as a tape player started singing its songs, old women and children began dancing; middle-aged women learned the response chorus after a few repetitions and joined in. Men gladly paid for the tapes. The songs spread like wildfire, even among groups heavily resistant to the gospel when presented in other media. Women in the Oku-Oku cult, forbidden to hear church preaching or become literate, learned these songs with Christian lyrics.

During moonlit nights, children sing the songs with gusto to accompany their jumping and clapping games. Everyone already expects some of the songs will be sung at the next big village dance.

Previously, Jesus was completely irrelevant to their lives. Now, they want to know more. The form of the message was so attractive and easy to use that they were drawn into its content.

The first duplication order of one hundred tapes sold out within a month (the time it took to arrive in all the Achoday villages), and more are being prepared.** Each tape costs more than a day's minimum wage.

Compare these exciting results to the Achoday long-standing literacy program: it takes two years to sell one hundred books, even when they are subsidized at one-tenth the cost of the cassette. Today among the Achoday, "buying" Scripture—through literacy—is as unappetizing as strange-tasting foreign foods. But offer Scripture songs and readings on cassette and they line up like we do at a pizza buffet. Make it good and hot, and they will pay for it, digest it, and come back for more.***

The Bible says, "Blessed are those who hear and obey." We cannot yet tell how many people have been persuaded to *obey* the word of God by these indigenous hymn cassettes. But we know that in only one month's time, the majority of Achoday people have *heard* some of the Word of God—without being literate or sitting in church. It's a great first step.

*Achoday is spelled Akyode in the orthography of Ghana.

**In partnership with Achoday musicians, composers, and singers, Paul and Linda Neeley eventually completed five different tapes. This story was written after producing the first tape.

***Since the publication of the Achoday New Testament, about seven years after this story was written, people became much more interested in obtaining the Word of God through literacy. Approximately ten percent of the people are now literate—a huge increase. Although it is still true that the majority of people may prefer to learn God's Word through oral means, the success of the literacy program has exceeded our expectations.

A version of this article also appeared in SIL's *Notes on Literature in Use and Language Programs*, September 1994.

Chapter 16

Ghana

Musical Midwives
by Sue Hall and Paul Neeley

Only the roar of a passing truck disturbed the moment of silence in the church. Men and women waited expectantly following the reading of a Scripture. And during that moment of silence, we wondered if this approach to making new Christian songs with nonreaders could really work. Then, hesitantly at first, but with growing confidence, one old woman began to sing out loud a song from her heart:

> He who is carrying a heavy load
> and is getting tired,
> bring it to Jesus. He will save you.
> You who labor hard, come to Jesus
> because he has peace.

As ethnomusicologists, we had come to coach representatives from various churches in the Vagla language area of Ghana, West Africa. Our goal was to develop indigenous hymnody—Christian music that would affirm these men and women's dual heritage as Vagla people and as children of God. We prayed for songs that would be scriptural, acceptable, and exciting both to unbelievers and Christians (a minority).

We served as "musical midwives," having made preparations (musical research), encouraged them to "push" (compose new songs), and helped in the final delivery (recording the new songs on cassette for future copying and distribution). Since not everyone at the workshop was literate, we had asked someone to read aloud a chosen passage from the Vagla New Testament—and waited.

As the old woman sang, 2000-year-old words tumbled out of her mouth, carried by a new melody composed in a traditional Vagla song type. Immediately the other women responded with the chorus. One of them picked up a rattle and provided accompaniment. Suddenly the dream in our minds of seeing Vaglas free to worship the true God through their own musical heritage became reality.

As the singer moved deeper into worshiping her Lord, she fell to her knees, singing, "Let's give him glory, because he is our Father." As she finished, another woman took up the theme in a different style of song. Then it was the men's turn, and soon all were up on their feet dancing in a circle or improvising an accompaniment on any rattles or drums available. Eager to sing and dance, they celebrated as people who were uniquely both Vagla and Christian.

Up until that day in 1997, the believers' worship music had been borrowed from other ethnic groups and was not rooted in Vagla culture, emphasizing the foreignness of their Christian expression. Now they had the musical resources to demonstrate how to sing as Christians and how to express it in a beautiful way that was natural for Vagla people, a way that would gain a hearing for the gospel from non-Christians. We, as guests, were privileged to serve as "midwives" at the exciting birth of a culturally-appropriate "heart music" that would be used in worship and evangelism by this people group.

Pastor Phillip, a Vagla blind man skilled in music of all kinds, testified to the power of these new songs composed in traditional styles. "You can't see my eyes because of these dark glasses, but when I started hearing these new songs, tears came. All these years, we could have been using our music to worship God and reach our people. Instead, it's been used by the devil. But now, now we can sing Bible verses!"

One of the verses, John 3:16, was accompanied by an ensemble of seven antelope horns played in intricate interlocking patterns. To the uninitiated, it sounds rather like a traffic jam; but to the Vagla people, it's one of the sweetest sounds on earth—especially when coupled with those life-changing words.

The Vagla musical types, *maara, zungo, dugu,* and others, are now being used to communicate the truth of the gospel in a form that all Vagla people instinctively recognize as their own. And it certainly sounds Vagla to our ears!

The seven thousand Vagla people of Ghana have had the New Testament in their language since 1977, yet the church has been slow to grow. "But now," as Pastor Phillip says, "I really hear God's words in these songs." So will many other Vaglas when they listen to the two, hour-long cassettes of Scripture songs and readings recorded over three days in an improvised studio at a church.

Late that evening, we met outside to eat pounded yam by starlight. After supper, more songs poured out. The two old women who were lead singers composed song after song as the night went on, extemporizing lyrics as their thoughts led them from the foundation of the initial Bible verse to other scriptural truths. The excitement spilled over in dancing and eagerness to be the next to sing.

That night we felt like floodwaters broke through a dam; like zero accelerated to eighty in five seconds. We felt the joy that fills our hearts when a loved one has been away a long time and then returns. It was a prelude to the joy of heaven with angels joining the crowd in singing:

> God loved the world so much
> that he gave his son Jesus,
> so let us believe in him, bow down before him
> and worship him.
> The Lord Jesus has called me,
> and I have come.

Another version of this article appeared in *Mission Frontiers*, 23:2, and a more detailed version appeared in *EM News*, 7:1. This version is published in a sample issue of *EthnoDoxology*, a music and missions journal.

Chapter 17

Ghana

Praising the High King of Heaven
by Paul Neeley and Sue Hall

Sheep and goats roam for food scraps; savannah dust blows where temperatures soar toward 40 degrees Celsius (100 degrees Fahrenheit), and a storm rumbles to the south. Despite such distractions, groups of Dagomba musicians attending a song-making workshop in a small village in Ghana are intent on their task—composing new songs in traditional music styles with words from their translated New Testament.

Each group reads a Bible verse chosen by the leader and then, hesitantly at first, develops it into a song lyric. Others add their voices; musicians bring their percussion and flute into the music, and a *bamaaya** song is given birth.

"This is the time when the kingdom of God is near," sings the leader.

The rest of the group picks up the refrain: "Repent and believe the good news."

A large crowd of observers from the village quickly gathers, women swaying to the music and children scrambling up trees for a better view. *What is this new thing? A bamaaya song that speaks of the kingdom of God and our need to repent and believe?*

Everyone likes bamaaya songs, old and young, educated and illiterate; even people from a major religion in the area pay attention to the content of the message because they thoroughly enjoy the form of the message. The whole community is hearing God's Word clearly, not only in their own language but also in music that reaches into their hearts like no other can. The message of God's kingdom is being made known through this indigenous Scripture song, one of almost three dozen new songs composed and recorded at the workshop.

The Dagomba people number between six and seven hundred thousand and live in over one thousand villages and a few larger towns. A majority claim some allegiance to the area's dominant religion; Christians make up less than 3 percent of the population. Churches are now seeing great value in using Scripture songs composed in local music styles to reach the more than one-half million Dagomba people, mostly non-literate, with the good news of the gospel.

After the first few songs were composed at the workshop, Pastor David Akonsi, a second generation Christian exclaimed, "When Christianity first came to our area of Ghana, we thought that using our own music was not appropriate to praise God. But now we see that if our church had started with the kind of indigenous music our people like, we would have made significant headway in reaching Dagomba communities."

For this one-day workshop, three experienced local composers led the fifty participants in making new songs. Each composer chose some Bible verses and then sat under a tree with their composing group.

First, they decided what part of the verse would be the choral response line; then the lead singer worked on fitting the rest of the verse between the response lines. With some practice, the groups could rough out a song in a few minutes. Then the song was revised and polished for half an hour or so.

Moses Yahaya Sheini, a Baptist pastor, led people in making new songs in the *simpa* style. To the accompaniment of frame drums and cowbell, they sang:

> Through Christ, God created everything,
> and God put all things into his hands
> (based on Colossians 1:16).

Michael Baba had previously recorded a cassette of passages from Genesis and Exodus, sung in the traditional style used by Dagomba praise singers, and accompanied by drummers. At this workshop, he decided to work in the musical genre of bamaaya, a very popular Dagomba dance used at various social occasions. To the interlocking percussion patterns of the *lunga* and *gungon* drums, his group sang:

> Jesus Christ was existing when nothing was there,
> and everything joined together in him
> (based on Colossians 1:17).

The third composer was Peter Denaba, an accomplished musician on the *gonje* fiddle, a single-stringed "bowed lute." The resonator, a half calabash, is covered with a monitor lizard skin; the string and bowstring are made of horsehair. To accompany that unique sound of horsehair bowed atop lizard skin, a song was created with these words based on Colossians 1:20:

> God reconciled everything to himself through Christ.
> He made peace with everything in heaven and on earth
> by means of his blood shed on the cross.

If you were a Dagomba person, can you imagine the power of hearing these words sung over and over to a Dagomba melody? The heart of the gospel now communicates in a form every Dagomba person is happy to hear! One man said, "I really admire the music. It's integrating Scripture into our Dagomba culture, and it will bring many people to hear the Word of God. The songs will cut across their unwillingness to listen to the gospel. If all churches would adopt this method, we would certainly see more people coming to Christ."

As the composing groups worked under three different trees, villagers came out to see music being created. Some two hundred people roamed among the musicians, waiting to see what would happen next. What an incredible way to get people to come and hear the Scriptures: pick a Bible verse, sit under a tree with your instrument and some friends, and two hundred people show up to listen to God's Word in song! The workshop coincided with a local feast day in this village, so the opportunity turned into an indigenous Christian music festival.

After each group had composed their first five songs, we gathered in the meeting room. Adults and children standing outside crowded together, filling every window and open door to watch. The villagers heard more Bible verses in this one day than in a month of Sunday services.

People were joyfully dancing in the aisles. Excitement hung in the air as thick as the dust being kicked up. As the gonje group sang about how "God was pleased to have all his fullness dwell in Christ" (Colossians 1:19), a dancer's large smock of midnight blue swirled around his knees above his intricate footwork. And God was pleased with that heartfelt Dagomba expression of worship as well.

The gonje fiddle and bamaaya drums are frequently used to praise Dagomba chiefs. Now they were being used to exalt the King of Kings. One woman said, "It's not only the chiefs of this world that are praised with our Dagomba drums and gonje; now we can also use our instruments to praise Naawuni (God, literally 'Chief of all gods')."

It touched our hearts deeply to see the impact of the songs on the believers, now freed to worship God with their unique cultural heritage. Moreover, it amazed us to see the attractiveness of these songs to those outside the Christian community. These songs will help the Christians fulfill their dual calling, not only to be worshippers but also to be witnesses to their own people as well.

During four days, the workshop participants composed thirty-three new Scripture songs. The last day, we recorded them on two one-hour-long cassettes, along with the Bible verses that inspired each song. Then, each singing group left the makeshift studio, wound through the village in joyous procession, and returned, playing their new songs: it was the local equivalent of a "March for Jesus"—with fifty children following them through the village.

One cassette had verses from different parts of the New Testament. The second contained songs and readings from the book of Revelation, such as this one based on Revelation 5:9:

> They sang a new song to the Lamb . . . you were slain,
> and with your blood you ransomed people for God
> from every tribe and language and people group and nation.

Yes, Christ also died for the more than one-half million Dagomba people of Ghana. A few of them know it already. And they want their brothers and sisters, their mothers and fathers, to share the joy of their salvation. Scripture songs will provide an irresistible invitation for many more to come dance and sing to the High King of Heaven.

Bamaaya is a suite of dances and associated musical patterns popular among the Dagomba.

A related longer article, "Report on the Dagomba Scripture Use Workshop," was published in *Notes on Sociolinguistics* 2:4, 1997.

Chapter 18

Senegal

Green Shoots in a Spiritual Desert
by Sue Hall

An older woman wakes up in the night, realizes her Savior has mercifully healed her, and sings the new song of thanksgiving he placed in her grateful heart.

A young man, formerly on the street as a religious beggar, draws on gifts inherited from his father and plays the melodic *tama*, an hourglass drum, as an accompaniment to simple songs of praise.

A Wolof-speaking pastor, gifted in guitar playing, gets excited at how effectively Wolof-style songs touch people's hearts in his neighborhood and composes more of them at a workshop.

Firstfruits of a harvest of Wolof believers, these diverse people are a tiny minority among the three to four million Wolof people who follow the major religion of Senegal. Like the new, bright green grass that comes up after the first rains, shoot by shoot in the Senegalese desert, flashes of color are appearing now in a spiritual desert. These believers, longing to see their friends and family come to know the Savior, are catching the vision of using their own music to worship Yàlla Aji Kawe Ji, the Most High God, and His Sent One, Yeesu.

Meetings

This growing group of songwriters gets together every three months in the capital city, Dakar. Wolof is the shared language for the many ethnic groups that have migrated there. Although most of the songwriters live in teeming Dakar and its suburbs (housing a fifth of the nation's population), occasionally a guest from a small, rural group of believers will travel in specially.

These believers, connected through the Wolof Music Commission,* meet in a church in the suburbs, tucked away from traffic noise. Meetings vary in form and size, with anywhere from three to fourteen participants, including up to three musically-gifted missionaries and facilitators. The majority are men in their twenties and thirties, with one older man attending irregularly. One older woman, with a clear gift for song making, is always there. Also, two younger women work on a new song or two even as they spend the morning cooking our lunch.

We begin the day with bread and coffee for breakfast, followed by a time of prayer, discussion of pressing issues, and sometimes a teaching-discussion on a biblical worship theme or an exploration of the question: "What *is* Wolof music?"

Then the drummers, guitarists, and singers pour themselves into creating new songs based on verses from the Bible or their own Christian experience. Because only the Wolof New Testament has been published in full, new song texts often draw on sayings and teachings of Jesus, how a disciple should live, festivals such as Christmas and Easter, and praise. Here is a song called "In Truth, Disciple!" about becoming disciples:

> Ci dëgg-dëgg taalibe
> Boroom bi def nuy taalibe, taalibe
> Boo nu defey taalibe
> Nu mën a dooni taalibe yu wóor a wóor

> Defal mag ñi taalibe
> Defal ndaw ñi taalibe, taalibe
> Boo leen defey taalibe
> Nu mën a dooni taalibe yu wóor a wóor

> Defal réew mi taalibe,
> Defal njiit yi taalibe, taalibe

Boo leen defey taalibe
Nu mën a dooni taalibe yu wóor a wóor

The Lord has made us disciples.
(Lord) If you make us disciples,
Then we can be true disciples.

(Lord) Make disciples of the old.
(Lord) Make disciples of the young.
(Lord) If you make them disciples,
Then they can be true disciples.

(Lord) Make the people of this nation, disciples.
(Lord) Make the leaders disciples.
(Lord) If you make them disciples,
Then they can be true disciples.

Composing Songs

Groups of at least three participants work on new compositions, often elaborating on an initial song idea brought by one of the groups, adding verses, instrumental accompaniments, and tweaking melodies and texts until the final product emerges. Composing these songs often depends on the right musicians showing up. The *kora*** is an especially nice accompaniment for longer narrative songs, but Christian players are few and far between.

Some of the participants have Western music training, while most play their instruments by ear. Few have much exposure or experience in the deep-rooted Wolof music traditions that are learned within the Wolof *géwél* musician's caste. Only one participant belongs to such a family.

The urban environment encourages fresh fusion sounds, blending traditions with modern instruments and beats such as *mbalax*.*** Even so, most have extensive exposure to Western and diverse African church music, and tend initially to compose in these styles. Some, whose mother tongue is not Wolof, prefer to write in the musical style of their own ethnic group. Therefore, even though the text is in Wolof, the music reflects the style of another people group, such as the Sereer.

As an ethnomusicologist, I encourage the group to rediscover their own traditional music and to listen with newly-attuned ears to the familiar descending melodies, call-and-response forms, and complex rhythms that shape Wolof music, including the urban fusions. As time goes on, they seem to be growing in confidence that true Wolof music styles can indeed be used for heart-felt worship or effective evangelism.

Recording

After our lunch break, an expatriate partner comes to record the morning's work with a basic field-recording set-up (cassette deck or laptop and four microphones). At this point, groups often lend musicians to each other in order to produce the best sound mix for the recording. Many songs can be recorded in either of two styles: Senegalese, or Western—whichever is preferred by the churches. The Christmas story and an account of Noah have employed long, spoken narrative interspersed with sung refrains.

The group's hope is to record an album for the mainstream Senegalese market, switching the style of some songs to an authentic Wolof sound. This poses recording challenges, however, because the needed multiple drumming parts can easily overwhelm the vocals on a non-multi-track recording.

The songs are collected on a master cassette until there are enough to fill an audiocassette. The group decides which ones to include, and then a local Christian studio produces it, along with a booklet in the liner notes, which provides all the song texts and biblical references.

The cassette production is well done, with good instrumental accompaniments such as the *jembe*,**** guitar, and keyboard; sometimes a kora and flutes are added. Unfortunately, the Dakar group tends to compose songs requiring these instruments, and it makes adapting the songs for less well-equipped groups challenging. Groups of believers outside the Dakar metropolis have access to fewer instruments and do not always have the skills to reproduce even the drumming portions of the songs.

Cassettes

Two cassettes, entitled "Praise Songs for the Lord," are intended for local Christians to use in sharing and teaching new songs to both literates and non-literates. Church music leaders select new songs to try in their congregations, which are usually a mixture of Senegalese and other nationalities. The songs are also disseminated outside Dakar to aid pioneer church planting among the Wolof. In isolated situations where the church is not yet established, these cassettes encourage seekers and new believers.

Wolof people do not always react positively to the cassettes. The songs contain possibly confusing terms such as "Son of God" and "life which does not end," and use an unfamiliar style influenced by Western, Sereer, or Central African urban churches. Therefore, Christian workers are selective about who receives or hears these cassettes.

The following song is important because it teaches the seven key aspects of God's character that are emphasized in chronological Bible storying, a teaching technique that is being used extensively to plant churches among the Wolof:

> Yàlla kenn la;
> Amul kenneen ku dul moom.
> Moom mooy sa Boroom
> Kon bul ko wutal moroom.
>
> Yàlla dafa jub.
> Yàlla xam na lépp.
> Yàlla moo di Aji Doole.
>
> Mbaax angi ciy moom.
> Bëggul bàkkaar.
> Yàlla lu mu dige, def ko.

God is One;
There is no one else besides Him.
He is your Lord
So don't go make any other equal to Him.

God is holy.
God knows everything.
God is all-powerful.

All goodness comes from Him.
He hates sin.
What God promises, He will do.

Senegalese Worship

Gradually, the dominance of European and West African styles of worship music is breaking down as Senegalese believers experience the joy of worshiping with their own popular *sabar* rhythms—the ultimate way to express joy in Wolof culture—and with Arab-influenced descending melodies that can be chanted devotionally as call-and-response. While urban churches still hesitate to include such music on a regular basis, the popularity of youth drummers' groups such as *Jii Gob* ("Sow and Reap") is making this old-new music increasingly acceptable as it is sung, drummed, and danced to the praise of Jesus Christ.

At a recent annual Wolof Consultation meeting, Jii Gob led the afternoon praise time. Two Gambian Christian "sisters" enthusiastically encouraged the conference participants in dancing to the glory of God as they called individuals to the front by tossing them a scarf. This was the first time sabar dancing had been seen in a "church" meeting, but even the most conservative Wolof Christian leaders joined in. The dances offered as worship were not the wild, sensual forms of sabar, but the more traditional, respectable yet energetic forms, still danced by older people at cultural events. The rhythms were purely Wolof, although played by hand and stick on jembes (already accepted for church worship) rather than on the more traditional sabar set of drums. The overall sound reflected contemporary Wolof *mbalax* music more than anything heard regularly in the churches—and many of the Wolof participants in the conference went away asking how this music could be used to glorify God in their different situations.

Two Christian recordings have been made of this mbalax music style: one by a church in The Gambia, which is proving very popular, though hard to obtain in Senegal; the other by a Dakar church some years ago. Initially meeting resistance, the Dakar church group disbanded, but new youth groups are picking up where the groundbreakers left off. They hope to produce albums that will reach into the marketplace with a powerful message—as well as rhythms that make you want to dance! Wolof dance styles are controversial, and it seems likely that only modified forms will make it into the church and Christian activities.

However, in addition to these animated songs, the Wolof Music Commission hopes to see the emergence of chants and simple songs that can be accessed easily by those without instrumental skills, especially in rural areas. Plans are underway to offer workshops all over Senegal and The Gambia so that urban musicians can meet with and encourage more isolated believers and model the process of making and using Wolof-style songs for worship and outreach.

The new songs that "taste Wolof" are spreading from the capital into desert regions of Senegal where small Wolof churches are beginning to spring up, searching for ways to worship that reflect their proud heritage. Psalm 147:7–8 declares,

> Sing to the LORD with thanksgiving; make music to our God
> on the harp.
> He covers the sky with clouds; he supplies the earth with rain
> and makes grass grow on the hills.

As a result of these workshops, we expect not only tender, green grass will grow, but also robust, lasting spiritual fruit as we work this ground faithfully and trust God's creative Spirit to water and enrich it.

*The Music Commission of the Wolof Consultation is an inter-church and inter-mission cooperation to reach the Wolof people with the good news.

**The *kora* is a 21-stringed harp originating in Mande people groups, but is appreciated by many other ethnic groups.

***The *mbalax* style is a fusion between traditional Wolof rhythms and vocal styles, and modern instruments (guitar, bass, keyboard, and others). It is extremely popular in Senegal and beyond.

****The *jembe* is a popular, West African goblet-shaped drum.

For more information about the Wolof Music Commission, you may contact Sue at suerachel@emailglobe.net or Mark Garrett at mncgarrett@sentoo.sn.

Chapter 19

Burkina Faso

Pirouetting toward Faith
by Colin and Dot Suggett
and Mary Hendershott

The elderly man heard the music and could no longer be content as a spectator. He just had to dance. With cane and pipe in hand, he joined a group of Turka Christians as they gave a spontaneous concert accompanied by *balafon** and *jembe.*** Women gathered around, offering the man encouragement. Finally, a cheer arose as the gentleman, smoke rising from his pipe, ended his dance with a full pirouette.

Thirty-five Turka Christians had gathered for a five-day workshop in the village of Moussodougou, Burkina Faso, to create brand-new worship songs based on biblical texts. "It was the highlight of the last three years, perhaps even the last ten," said Dot and Colin Suggett, Wycliffe team leaders for the Turka translation project. "The excitement and synergy of having such a large group of Turka Christians together with such a *fun and noble* purpose was evident from the start."

Under the direction of Mary Hendershott, Wycliffe ethnomusicologist, the group discussed how traditional Turka instruments and music styles could be used to worship God. Participants then formed groups and composed a song based on a specific Bible text. Within an hour, diverse melodies began to emerge. This pattern continued throughout the week, and by Saturday, sixteen new songs had been composed.

A friendly neighbor's newly built mud-brick house served as a makeshift studio. The musicians squeezed into the tiny room filled with musical instruments and recording equipment, but even this did not quell their enthusiasm. Throughout the day each composing group recorded their new songs as well as Scripture readings. As the familiar Turka melodies accompanied by balafon, jembe, and flute floated outside, those waiting their turn in the "studio" broke into a very quiet but spontaneous dance. Their joy was infectious.

On Saturday evening, the musicians agreed to stay longer than planned and the concert moved "to the streets" just outside the church building. The music, dance, and singing attracted considerable attention from vendors returning from the village market. Folks were drawn by the familiar melodies, but didn't know what to make of the refrain: "Who can forgive sins, if not Jesus alone?"

Who is this Jesus anyway? they must have wondered.

The twentieth-century Christian expositor A.W. Tozer wrote, "A church is strong or weak just as it holds to a high or low idea of God. . . . A believer's faith can never rise higher than his conception of God. . . . An inadequate conception of God must result in a weak faith."****

The faith of the Turka church has risen skyward by composing these new Scripture songs. Previous to the workshop, the church music repertoire did not communicate a complete conception of God. These new songs, however—embraced enthusiastically by everyone—are based on solid teaching from the Word of God. Themes such as God's love, goodness, justice, mercy, and His saving power emerge with quiet and refreshing authority that accompanies biblical truth. Jesus' ethical teachings, such as loving and forgiving one's enemies, tower above the petty dos and don'ts of the church's old repertoire. As a result, God is greatly honored, and people's faith is strengthened.

Tozer concluded, "Faith comes effortlessly to the heart as we elevate our conceptions of God by a prayerful digestion of his Word. And such faith endures, for it is grounded upon the Rock."****

In a primarily oral society, how does the average man, woman, and child "prayerfully digest" the Word of God? It begins when Scripture, translated into the mother tongue, provides lyrics for new songs, sung over and over, laying a foundation of biblical knowledge. Faith enters the heart, seemingly effortlessly, and the church grows, grounded on Jesus the Rock.

And just as important, others in the community, like the pirouetting man, are drawn by the music and confronted with the eternal truths of God's Word.

*A *balafon* is a xylophone-type instrument with gourd resonators.

**The *jembe* is a popular, West African footed drum.

***A. W. Tozer and Harry Verploegh, *The Set of the Sail* (Christian Publications, 1986), chapter 10.

Chapter 20

Panama

Spirit-Converted Songs:
Lullaby, Prayer, and Folk Dance
by Ron Binder

"We can't use our music; it's bad. If we do, everyone will think we're drunk."

The first Christian Wounaan people living in the tropical forest of southeast Panama balked at using their indigenous music for Christian worship. They told me and my wife, Kathy, that of their various song styles, the "lullaby"* was traditionally sung when drunk.

The Wounaan claimed they could express themselves more freely when inhibitions were lowered by cane liquor. When drunk and singing this style, young men or women would often extol the virtues of someone of the opposite sex, or a spouse. A woman, for example, would sing about how she feels protected and secure because her husband provides for her and the children; he's such a good hunter and always brings back meat; he builds houses well or carves out canoes beautifully; he always gets them safely to their destination when they travel. Such laudable and pleasing lyrics seemed adaptable to praising God—except for the problem of drunkenness. . . .

In 1993, Wycliffe ethnomusicologist Tom Avery, accompanied by a Discovery** team of student musicians, held a workshop for Wounaan*** and three other languages. One goal was to help each language group write a description of their own musical styles, associated beliefs, and ceremonies. Tom discussed with them the implications of Ephesians 5:18–20:

> Do not get drunk on wine, which leads to debauchery. Instead,
> be filled with the Spirit. Speak to one another with psalms,
> hymns and spiritual songs. Sing and make music in your
> heart to the Lord, always giving thanks to God the Father for
> everything, in the name of our Lord Jesus Christ.

It was a turning point for Christian Wounaan thinking. They understood that people shouldn't sing because they're drunk, but because God's Spirit now lives in them and singing is a way to respond to God from the heart.

Following the workshop, one of the participants wrote a book in Wounaan on their music styles, describing the ceremonies associated with their six musical genres and their cultural implications. Sample transcriptions and a cassette tape were included. The book was later translated into Spanish and English. A booklet of Tom's teachings, illustrated by musical clips on an accompanying cassette was also published.

In 1996, at the first Wounaan hymn writers workshop, a songbook of eighteen new hymns and an accompanying recording were produced. Most of the compositions "converted" songs traditionally sung during drinking fests. Here are the translated lyrics of one of these lullaby hymns:

> In the past when I didn't know God's Word,
> I would just do any old thing [immoral, purposeless living]
> because I was so stubborn.
> But today since his Spirit has spoken, as it were, to my heart,
> I've become really happy.
> Since that day, I have gotten really good thoughts—thoughts
> that are new.
> When we're like that, we will walk forever with God.
> Never looking back, always walking with Him.

After the workshop, everyone, including a Discovery team that had assisted the participants, went to a village where a Wounaan pastor introduced the new books and hymns at a "town" meeting. The Discovery students participated too by singing a couple of the songs in Wounaan, and the people went wild!

Copies of the hymn cassettes spread quickly from house to house and village to village. When the new songs were first introduced in one village, church attendance was typically about twenty-five. The week after these new songs were introduced, it shot up to over one hundred people. The pastor encouraged the congregation to keep composing— although, over time, the catalyst of a workshop proved necessary.

A second hymn writer's workshop for five participants was held in July 2005 and lasted three weeks. Other genres besides the lullaby were focused on, and original composition was encouraged. A traditional prayer style, once at the heart of Wounaan culture, was part of a ceremony using a large canoe-shaped instrument, accompanied by antiphonal singing by women and various kinds of flutes played by men. Unfortunately, in the past, missionaries ignored or even discouraged this style, but in this workshop, two compositions used it.

Another song style for dedicating a new house to God was used to create one hymn.

A folk dance style, imitating animals and folk heroes, served well for a hymn written for children.

A couple of hymns were written in the lullaby style and borrowed from existing tunes.

Other songs drew on popular Latino styles: *cumbia, vallenato,* and *ranchera.* Three tunes were composed by a Wounaan who plays classical guitar, and attends the conservatory of music in Panama City. Although these classical sounding tunes are admirable, to us, the lyrics seem forced.

In this workshop, participants produced twenty-eight hymns. Combined with the original lullaby hymn collection, booklets and tapes of all the hymns were sent to the four Wounaan churches in Panama City and to twelve churches in Wounaan villages.

Two weeks after the workshop, the Wounaan presented the new hymns at one of their churches in Panama City. About 250 people attended, representing all the churches in the city. People jumped up out of their seats at hearing some of the songs. I've never seen them so animated before. Spontaneous clapping erupted several times and even some hooting and hollering during the Latino-style hymns.

When the children's folk-dance style was played and sung, the congregation demanded an encore as children lined up and performed their "butterfly dance" to an adoring crowd.

In the lullaby style, a long falsetto tone often prefaces the song proper. One elderly man said, "When I heard that first note, I closed my eyes, and it brought me back to my childhood. God must really enjoy hearing these songs."

The prayer-ceremony-style hymn evoked this comment from some of the women: "When we heard the melancholic tones of the singer and responded (antiphonally) to each phrase, we became reflective and sensed the presence of God."

A ranchera-style hymn, giving a personal testimony made one man say: "That's so true! I could sing *my* story like that!"

All who attended the service received booklets and recordings of the hymns. Also each of the churches in remote villages received them through the mail.

Thanks to these new hymn creations, Wounaan songs now get equal time in churches, along with translated western and Latino hymns. Also, Wounaan-style hymns have become the method of choice for evangelism. Because some of these music styles have not been used much for years, everyone wants to hear and try singing them.

Released from their inhibitions, not through drink, but through the Spirit, Wounaan are freely and joyfully extolling the attributes of a faithful God. Non-Christians, as well, are discovering the gospel through song. To the great delight of the Wounaan, and to ours, now no one would even think to say Wounaan music is bad! No, it's not bad at all.

*The "lullaby" style was so named because that's what it sounds like to the Binders.

**Discovery* trips are designed for 21–35 year olds who are serious about missions and would consider working with Wycliffe long-term, but want to experience what it's really like before completing their training/education. Trips typically last about seven weeks. See http://www.wycliffe.org/discovery/home.htm.

***The population of the Wounaan is about seventeen thousand.

Chapter 21

Papua New Guinea

Singing Literacy Classes
by Carol Brinneman with Mark Hepner

Wouldn't anyone jump at the chance to learn to read? Not always. In cultures where oral communication has sufficed for centuries, the hard work of mastering a new way is a challenge for many. Singing literacy lessons proved helpful for the approximately five thousand Bargam people of Papua New Guinea (PNG), an island nation north of Australia.

Wycliffe translator Mark Hepner and co-translator Lazarus Tumuw decided to read several Scripture passages in the Bargam language onto cassette tape to help people learn to read the newly translated New Testament more fluently. People could then look up the passage being read and follow along, seeing the words as they heard them.

At the same time, one of the Bargam language committee members developed an interest in collecting Bargam worship songs from different villages. So Mark borrowed a mini-disc recorder and recorded eleven songs in the first village—and interspersed them among the New Testament readings, producing a 90-minute tape. The response to the tape was enthusiastic, and the initial, tentative run of fifty copies was not nearly enough to satisfy the demand. In the end, Mark, with the help of the PNG Non-print Media Department, produced and sold over two hundred copies of this Scripture and song tape.

In the months following the New Testament dedication, a one-day "Use Your Bible Course" was held in nine villages. Several times, while the team sat around waiting for folks to show up, they started playing the tape. This always evoked much interest, and songbooks were usually handed out to those listening. People immediately started following along in the songbook in order to learn the songs.

Mark says, "The people love the songs. We even hear folks singing the new songs around the village, not just in church!"

Those first-taped songs sparked interest in other villages that wanted their songs recorded too. Mark happily continued taping. As a result, they produced 200 copies of a song book in *Tokples* (that is, "talk of the place" or "vernacular") containing 36 worship songs, as well as 100 copies of the accompanying song tape.

Seeing how much interest the music generates, Mark has come to realize that a musical component in literacy classes would provide a great introduction to reading. People enjoy singing so much; it is a highly motivational tool.

Mark says, "The tapes were way more popular than I ever dreamed they would be. Perhaps we didn't realize so many people would have easy access to tape players. We believe these tapes will be used to increase reading fluency as well as encourage people to use their mother tongue in every aspect of their spiritual lives."

This article has been adapted from "In Papua New Guinea: recordings, literacy, song" posted on wycliffe.org in March 2004.

Chapter 22

Northeast India

Poetic Reflections on Scripture:
Dawn in Northeast India
by Michael T. Heneise

Beautiful and haunting, the sounds wafted into my New Delhi hotel room night after night. Only a few yards away, a local mosque reverberated in Ramadan celebration. I would wake up at two or three in the morning for a glass of water and discover the mosque resonant with worship—and it never stopped.

Having just concluded teaching at the Worship and Music Conference sponsored by the Council of Baptist Churches of Northeast India, this continuous worship led me to ponder what I had just experienced with my students.

Held within the ancient Baptist missionary compound at Nagaon, Assam, the conference was attended by about five hundred participants from scores of distinct communities, coming from both the plains and the surrounding Himalayan hills. The awesome display of wealth in colors, traditions, and languages represented clear examples of God's infinitely diverse and beautiful handiwork and creativity. Even though the echoes of time-worn missionary-translated hymns could almost be heard in the various bungalows and school-houses built in the early-to-mid 1800s, I found this an ideal setting for a workshop on indigenous song writing.

The perfectly preserved compound sat peacefully in the center of the bustling town around it, and as time stood still, I imagined the early missionaries' first encounters with the various indigenous communities in the surrounding mountains. What had it been like to be among the first Christians from the outside world to experience the colorful, melodious festivals of the Garo or Naga communities?

I witnessed a different kind of celebration in one of my ethnodoxological workshops where we keenly felt the presence of the Holy Spirit. A young woman from the district of Karbi Anglong (Assam), after some basic instruction and much encouragement, sang a song she had composed in class. Roselyn Taropi's voice glided effortlessly through the words of her testimony set to a Karbi folk melody:

> De kardom, denta O Hemphu! Dan taike derni dzir pover . . .
> Hear my prayer, Oh Lord! Hear the cry of my heart . . .

Interweaving her poetry with carefully selected Scripture texts her group had just reflected upon, she created a song that spoke of God's deliverance and healing in her life. In this Spirit-charged atmosphere, participants from Assam, Meghalaya, Manipur, and Nagaland stood and testified, one after another, to God's transforming power in their lives. They told their stories in their own tongues, using melodies born in their own hearts, contexts, and traditions. Among the Manipuris, five different communities speak five distinct languages. Among the Nagas, there were Aos, Angamis, Sumis, Tangkhuls, and Konyaks. We indeed witnessed an astonishing and diverse worship of nations, tongues, and tribes! The beautiful singing and sharing of these newly composed worship songs blessed everyone tremendously.

Many had never experimented with re-reading Scripture texts in a group context with the intention of creating poetic reflections set to music for the purpose of worship. Scripture texts came alive in idioms that had deep meaning in their cultures and contexts. Powerful testimonies resounded with biblical stories of miraculous deliverance from sickness, evil spirits, and death itself. The communities had now found a voice through which to develop, experiment with, dialogue about, and present theology in its primary form of expression: worship. As the well-known Asian theologian Choan Seng Song writes:

Theology is poetry of God in the prose of the people. It is God's hymn in the songs of men, women, and children. It is God's story in parables and folktales of our brothers and sisters. Theology is God's mask dance* played in the mask dance of those who, in the darkness of night, long for the approach of dawn.**

Throughout our time together, the participants' freedom to worship God in new ways grew significantly. In fact, at the end of the conference, while many waited for their buses to take them back into deep mountains and distant villages, an impromptu circle dance began. I too was suddenly swept up in the dance, and having familiarized myself with the sounds and pronunciation of much of my students' poetic reflections, I found myself singing five or six of the newly composed indigenous worship songs with them.

I have continued to meet with many of the original students from the Nagaon conference. Many of them have earnestly taken on the task of revitalizing their local church worship through newly composed worship songs. Roselyn Taropi, for example, has composed and recorded two CDs for her community and for radio. The very first song she created in the workshop has become an anthem, of sorts, for my workshops on indigenous worship composition. For example, in a workshop in Sarajevo, Bosnia, it served as an example of indigenous folk melodies that can be used to create new worship songs among new believers from various religious backgrounds.

Indigenous composition has proved a powerful vehicle for a community to see Christ revealed and engaged in the struggles of their own context. Moreover, it has taught Christians to express their faith in the most visible, tangible, and perhaps the most powerful medium—worship. The light-infusing songs created by the Spirit, through these believers, compete with the haunting melodies of the night. May their transforming power continue until the light of dawn shines brightly.

*Contrasting with H. Richard Niebuhr's thesis of Christ as transformer of culture, C.S. Song's theology is centered in the idea of Christ "fulfilling" culture. This he does by finding God's imprint and life-giving presence reflected in the cultural expressions of the Asian community. In the phrase, "Theology is God's mask dance played in the mask dance," Song is essentially saying that Jesus—Emmanuel, meaning "God with us"—was always present in Asia; although He was not fully revealed, He eagerly awaited the time He would be.

**Choan Seng Song, *Theology from the Womb of Asia*. Maryknoll: Orbis Books, 1986. p. 227.

Movement 2:
Suffering,
Persecution, Healing

Chapter 23

Sudan

Dinka Worship:
Keeping Strong in the Midst of Persecution
by Frank Fortunato

The door was closed and fans switched off . . . the tiny room instantly became an oven.

A large set of drums recently moved into the room now serving as a recording studio had drastically reduced available floor space. Undaunted, eighteen Sudanese Dinka choir members managed to squeeze in.

Once the drumming and singing began, the choir became oblivious to their surroundings: the recording equipment; the four strangers from Heart Sounds International (HSI) busy audiotaping, videotaping, and snapping photos. Hour after hour, the Dinka sang medley after medley, and though drenching in perspiration, they sang with vigorous abandon, taking only short breaks to cool down, get a drink, or munch a sandwich. The choir knew their songs well, and most were recorded in one take. In all, thirty-three songs and almost eighty minutes of worship music were recorded in one day.

The African nation of Sudan has suffered unspeakably. War waged against the Christian and animist south resulted in two million dead. The devastation included pillage, rape, people sold into slavery, and whole villages burned. Many of the survivors huddled into refugee camps at the borders of Uganda and Kenya, while millions more melted into the outskirts of greater Khartoum, the tri-city capital complex. Of all the people groups undergoing persecution, none has been more devastated than the Dinka.

Christian ministries have responded to this present-day holocaust, sending in food, clothing, money to free the slaves, and other forms of relief and aid. Another Christian response has been an effort to strengthen believers by encouraging their worship through this time of deep trial. Christian radio ministries have targeted broadcasts in the various languages of Sudan.

In late February 2002, HSI sent a diverse team to Khartoum. The musicians included a commercial airline pilot who helped get cheap standby tickets for most of the trip. Another spoke fluent Arabic and even some Dinka, greatly facilitating the communications. Another had written film scores and recorded projects in different parts of the world, including assignments for national television. I, as team leader, brought almost three decades of music ministry to the mix, including previous trips to Khartoum.

On arrival, we discovered the room we had expected to use was no longer available. They took us to a smaller one at a larger church. Mattresses had been purchased and cleverly framed to form freestanding units to prohibit outside noises and deaden sounds from bouncing around the makeshift studio room. Recording began with a Sudanese worship leader using a sophisticated auto-accompaniment keyboard, brilliant in his ability to manipulate the various styles that changed continually.

Nevertheless, we began to wonder why we came all the way to Africa to record rhythms and sounds we hear every day on radio in our own backyards. But later, as the vocals were added, these songs took on an interesting hybrid, urban-Afro sound, punctuated by gutsy Arab phrases.

Two other youth bands recorded over the next two days. They also chose to record their urban-Arab arrangements. When we asked about their *ethnic* background and music, they admitted they just didn't relate to those music structures.

Another Sudanese brother, however, from the Nuba Mountains, was eager to share and record his local music. He was one of the students who attended the music writing class the HSI team taught. He brought his handmade harp, "hardwired" to the Nuba pentatonic (five-note) scale. We captured some of his songs on the spot with our back up battery-powered, digital equipment.

We met many other musicians from various Sudanese people groups at the conferences and church meetings where our HSI team ministered. Having heard so much about the suffering and persecution of the Dinka, however, our team particularly targeted recording this group. We reserved the final day to record the worship of one of the Dinka churches.

And it was there that we four "strangers" met in that tiny, stifling hot room with those eighteen choir members. Having expected to record five to six songs and planning for a half dozen singers, we were delightfully surprised when that large choir showed up. Perplexed, we wondered, *How would we ever squeeze a whole choir into the tiny studio makeshift studio?* But none of this bothered the Dinka. And, rather than coming armed with five to six songs, the leader told us they had at least thirty songs ready to sing!

During a brief rehearsal, we discovered they sang mostly in unison and to the accompaniment of two drummers playing various polyrhythms. Before long, the recording marathon began. The choir divided their songs into various medleys, and punctuated the start and ending of each song with a hearty shout of "Hallelu-Hallelujah!"

On the final medley, some of the teenage girls could not resist adding their local dance steps, and began moving about the cramped studio. Soon the older women joined in with their swaying. Before we knew what was happening, all the ladies joyously circled the tiny room, while the men jumped vigorously in place. A delightful pandemonium erupted as the choir praised, danced, and marched, oblivious to cables, stands, mics, whatever. One engineer quickly put down his digital camera and rushed through the circle to grab the microphone stands lest they fall over as the choir continued in their exuberant, abandoned worship.

In the aftermath, we videotaped the leader and, through translation, asked him the meanings of the songs. They spoke of their difficult situation in life, but also expressed hope, faith, joy, and trust in the Lord.

These were the very people whose children had been abducted and sold into slavery, whose women had been raped, houses burned, and crops and cattle destroyed. To see these persecuted believers overflow with worship was a highlight of the trip—despite the challenge of recording the last medley of songs.

We realized afresh that—through worship—God keeps his people strong in times of difficulty and persecution. We vividly experienced the theme that drives all we do in Heart Sounds International: "Every people should worship our awesome God in an awesome way that reflects their own culture."

As we pondered such an unforgettable moment, we imagined angels reserving front row seats, as they get ready for vigorous Dinka worship around the throne. The four of us on the HSI team have ordered our tickets for front row box seats, as well. The suffering Sudanese believers made us homesick for heaven.

Heart Sounds International is a fellowship of volunteer musicians and recording engineers who take ten-day mission trips to an area to teach on biblical worship and train believers in various music skills, as well as record indigenous worship songs. HSI volunteers see themselves as frontline missionaries whose tools include cables, microphones, plug adapters, and state-of-the-art digital equipment. Each HSI trip, so far, has comprised one to six people who raise funds for their travel, donate their time and services, and even fund the purchase of complete digital recording facilities that are left behind in places where local musicians are ready to record. HSI projects link with many evangelical agencies and churches and are coordinated by the music director of Operation Mobilization.

Since the first trip made in 1999, HSI teams have gone mostly to places where no Christian recording facilities exist or where it is prohibitive for believers to go to commercial studios. Past recordings have all been non-western and non-English, with a particular focus on capturing the indigenous "heart language and music" of local believers. In some areas, these efforts resulted in the very first professionally recorded worship CDs, the first Christian studios set up, and the first songbook resources produced. The recorded songs have been broadcast by missionary radio or satellite TV programs.

Each HSI project takes months of preparations, identifying a local organizer, a music coordinator, and defining the goals and activities for each visit. Local believers prepare a demo tape of the 10–12 songs the HSI team will record, along with a rough translation of those songs. Another requirement is the preparation of a room (wall-to-wall and floor-to-ceiling blankets do just fine) that will serve as the recording venue. Before leaving for trips, the recording team prepare themselves by listening to web radio of the region, studying the culture, music, church situation, and so forth.

Chapter 24

Sudan

"God Looks Back on Us":
Healing Songs for a Suffering Nation
by Karen Campbell

"Where is God in all of this?" was the question on everyone's lips. Southern Sudan had suffered brutally under civil war for decades. Instead of leaving this question to evaporate on the African plains, Stephen Diit, a Dinka, answered with a vision of healing for the Sudanese church. Diit decided to form a song-making group within his home congregation. He named it *Jol Wo Lieec*, "God, look back on us."

Many persecuted Sudanese Christians believed God had forgotten them, just as the Western world had ignored their plight. But Stephen encouraged his friends to write laments and other songs and cry out to God to remember them, to "look back over his shoulder" at their pathetic state. What resulted was unprecedented. Very soon, nearly every Episcopal church in southern Sudan had formed a Jol Wo Lieec group. During the 1980s, revival broke out among the churches, and people made pilgrimages from one village to the next, singing songs composed by Jol Wo Lieec groups.

My husband and I heard about the richness of these songs and were eager to hear and understand them for ourselves. Having worked in the music department at Daystar University in Nairobi since 1998, I often taught Sudanese refugees. One of my first encounters was with Mary, a very tall, elegant Dinka lady. She had composed numerous songs in her language, and when she sang them, we knew she could move any heart. Her hymns were powerful, high-text, and metaphor-laden, sharply contrasting with the repetitive Kiswahili choruses we sang in Kenyan churches.

At the same time, I read a book written by Marc Nikkel, an American missionary who spoke Dinka fluently and had collected and studied thousands of their songs. He had spent years with the Dinka at a time when most missionaries, because of political instability, only spent weeks with them. At one point, he was captured by the rebel SPLA army and trekked with them for over 150 miles—all the while learning their songs and idioms. Marc was deeply entrenched in the culture, and his writing inspired me. When he died in 2000 after a long battle with cancer, I sensed a need to keep his legacy alive. That pushed me, in part, to go to a UN refugee camp at Kakuma to collect songs for myself.

At Easter 2001, my husband David and I traveled to the camp, which lies on the border between Sudan and Kenya. Our plan was to lead a music workshop: teaching the Dinka Christians some basic Western music skills—theory and keyboard—in exchange for sharing their songs with us.

That's where we met Stephen Diit and learned about the Jol Wo Lieec groups. We were amazed to see how highly developed these song groups had become. Each group is divided into four branches: a branch of composers; a branch of musicians and evangelists; one called "the final discussion," which looks for points of commonality between their culture and Christianity; and finally, the "tunemakers" responsible for collecting the songs composed, interpreting them properly, and appropriating them for church use.

Symbols: the Cross

Dinka songs exhibit an exciting, indigenous quality in the way they employ cultural symbols. The cross, in particular, is one powerful

Christian symbol that has been brought into their culture in a unique way. In one of their songs, they sing:

> The cross on which Christ was nailed is the centerpost;
> It stands between the evil Jok and the believer.

The Dinka people are pastoral; cattle are dominant in their culture. In the cattle camp, the centerpost is the pivot of activity. Also, in every person's house, there is a central post that is the supporting pillar of the house. Every cow in the cattle camp has its own central stick or post where it will rest at the end of each day. Therefore, the cross for the Dinka has now become their "centerpost," giving them support and direction.

While in the refugee camp, we witnessed a worship service where most of the men and women held long, ebony wooden crosses as they sang, pulsing them up and down to the rhythm of the music. Throughout the camp, Christians walk everywhere carrying their crosses so that if anyone is in trouble, they can spot a Christian who would help and offer them shelter. Christian families used to erect a cross at the top of their houses to identify them as a sure place of refuge.

The Blood

Another powerful image recurring in songs was shed blood. Traditionally, a person was reconciled to another by sacrificing a cow; shed blood ensured forgiveness. Also, cleansing from guilt came from blood sprinkled over a guilty party. Blood also possessed healing powers. A Dinka man would traditionally put blood on his doorpost in order to protect his family from illness. And a drop of chicken's blood put in the mouth of a sick person served as healing medicine. These different powers of blood carry over into Christianity, as we see in the following song:

> Let's drink the blood of Jesus
> To wash sin out of our own heart.
> It is the Lamb of God; the Lamb
> By whom we are redeemed.

We shall never again have to sacrifice to Jok.
There is no other sacrifice.

—Michael Ayuen Deng

The opening lines begin with the strong image of drinking the blood of Jesus in order to wash all infirmities from the heart. It connects—spiritually—with the ceremony of putting blood in a sick person's mouth for healing. The Dinka have thus powerfully incorporated their faith into their way of life without compromising either.

Jok

Encouraging Dinka to turn from *Jok* was one of Jol Wo Lieec's major goals in song making. Jok is a traditional spirit to which Dinka offer sacrifices, asking for protection of their cattle. In the song above, they recognize Jesus as their final and only needful sacrifice. This next song shows the vanity of sacrificing to Jok, which results in nothing more than feeding termites and insects.

> We have something to say, Let's say it!
> We have something to convey, Let's convey it!
> Don't worship the homes of animals, you will be burnt.
> Why do you worship homes and not God?
> We worship the Father in heaven.
> You give the earth food—who will eat it?
> When you come back, you will find it
> already eaten by the termites.
> Why do you feed insects?
>
> . . .
>
> Don't cheat, this displeases a person's heart, eee!
> Then God will turn his face away from you.
> God wants us to do his work;
> Christ wants us to do his work.

The Son of God said the true shining light
has come into our hearts. Father, we look to
you in prayer—see that the true light has come
into our hearts.

—Michael Cieng Garang, 1999

One final song resembles Western psalms that petition God:

We praise you, O God of generations,
for you have called us into your kingdom.
Our God, you love us; even though we fall into sin,
You should not leave us at all.
Teach us your words, Lord of peace.

—Solomon Machar Tuch, 1998

Dinka believers place high value on God's continual presence with them. The traditional Jok was perceived as distant and inscrutable, only listening to people in times of emergencies. But God comes near and continues to love people in spite of their sin. This is the God who has truly "looked back over his shoulder" and remembered Sudanese Christians.

The Dinka have endeavored to incorporate these three major themes—the cross, blood and Jok—in their songs in culturally-appropriate ways. The cross is a Christian symbol that has been brought into the culture and assimilated. Blood, covenant, and sacrifice are elements already present in the culture but have found correspondence with similar themes in Christian culture. Finally, Jok, a divinity from their culture, has no correspondence with Christian faith and so is rejected, and even derided.

Dinka crosses are made of ebony and decorated with pieces of metal scavenged from the ground—actually, broken gunshells. What a powerful image these crosses are, symbolizing what the Dinka are achieving through their songs and faith. The Dinka exist in a strife-ridden war zone and yet they choose to "beat" the tools of war into instruments fit to articulate their suffering and their trust in God. He did not turn his back on them. Rather he has come near to give them fresh courage and hope.

Chapter 25

Estonia

"We Sang Ourselves Free":
Music Lessons from Estonia
by Steven Pierson

As I looked over the ship's railing, the day dawned with a gray hue on the Baltic horizon. When the Estonian coastline appeared, I felt a tinge of apprehension in my heart, wondering why I was making this trip in the first place. And as the ship approached the dock, I realized I was on my way to what was then part of the Soviet Union—and no turning back.

The port was as I expected, gray and dirty with pushy guards, backed by machine guns and unfriendly dogs. After papers, visas, checks, and questions, we were allowed into the city of Tallinn. As soon as we passed the doorway into the street, everything changed. An Estonian pastor greeted us kindly, inquiring about our trip and if we had enough rest and food. Quite unexpectedly, a feeling of warmth and familiarity came over me.

After a brief meal, we went to the church. It was older, small, and plain with unfinished wooden floors and pews. The number of people in attendance was, again, a surprise. I had been led to believe that few people attended church in Estonia, yet this church was filled to capacity. I also had the notion that only the poor and outcasts attended church, but in contrast, most of the people I spoke with were intelligent, articulate, and well educated.

I had taken along my French horn to play if the opportunity arose. I remember thinking it would probably be in vain because no one would have the piano skills necessary to accompany the pieces I brought. To my delight, I soon found out that nothing was further from the truth.

As I entered the door of the church, there stood a pleasant Estonian woman. She introduced herself as the church pianist, and I gave her the music. She took a brief look at it and then said, "No problem." I stood there in shock, wondering if she actually realized the difficulties in the piano accompaniment for a Mozart Horn Concerto.

After hearing her play a few notes, it became abundantly clear that she was a highly trained and sensitive pianist; in fact, she is still one of the most impressive accompanists I have ever heard. She handled the difficult parts at full tempo with ease and elegance, never missing a note on the out-of-tune, old upright piano in the sanctuary. Of all the times I had performed this Mozart concerto, this proved one of the most special.

I also discovered that the Mozart was not the only piece of serious music scheduled for the worship service that morning. A violin-viola duet by Bach and some of the most beautiful and skillful choral singing I had ever heard were also included. My astonishment grew with each passing note of music. I had come to Estonia to minister in music; instead, I was the one being ministered to while I listened with surprise and delight.

On my trip back to Sweden, I began to ponder the significance of this musical atmosphere. I had expected the physical poverty of Eastern Europe to be accompanied by artistic and spiritual poverty. I found just the opposite to be true. In Sweden, many people enjoy great material wealth and religious freedom but endure an emotional void and spiritual poverty that defies explanation.

In Estonia, Christian youth ministry was prohibited for over fifty years; Christians were systematically discriminated against and often outright persecuted. Bibles were scarce and Christian literature virtually non-existent. All of this led my Western-trained mind to conclude that without these crucial means for ministry, no real ministry could exist. Christian growth would be stymied, if not altogether prevented, I thought.

Yet my observations in Tallinn supported quite a different conclusion. The Christians in Estonia were filled with a life and spiritual energy not visible in Sweden. My mind began to wonder if my concepts of ministry were too narrow and if there was a connection between the Christian vitality I observed and the depth of the music I experienced.

Formal Research

Years later, while engaged in doctoral studies, these questions once again occupied my thinking. I wondered if a firm link could be discovered between participation in music ministry and tangible overall Christian development. Most Christians may intuitively presume such a link exists. However, there is little serious research to confirm this specific cause-effect relationship, particularly in a situation in which Christianity is systematically repressed. One thing was clear in my mind, however. If such a link exists, Estonia would be a place to find it.

After I assembled a theoretical base, my doctoral committee created a series of research goals that could potentially answer this overall question. These goals included simply asking Estonian Christians to express their perspective on musical experience as it relates to Christian ministry. We were also particularly interested in how musical experience revealed, illustrated, and related to the Estonian cultural and Christian identity. In addition, there was also a desire on the part of my committee to examine any changes that were occurring in the music of local churches since independence (1991), and the effect these changes were having on Christian development.

I set out again for Estonia, armed with these questions, hoping that people would be willing to respond and give me some basic answers. When I arrived, I was greeted by winter, complete with six inches of ice from a recent storm. Snow clearing equipment was scarce, so deep ruts scarred the side roads. I stayed with a well known composer who filled my "free" hours with numerous stories about composers, music, and life in the era of the Soviet Union, especially during World War II and under Stalin's rule.

To obtain the best information available, I recruited a team of translators to help with communicating and transcribing the interviews. In all, our team conducted twenty-four interviews with pastors and church musicians from various parts of the country over the course of about six weeks. Each interview lasted several hours, followed by furious typing to transcribe the material into written form. Once finished, this written data became the basis for the analysis and conclusions.

After two months of reading and thinking through the mountain of material we had gathered, the broader subject categories became obvious. Our interviews revealed highly detailed and well supported opinions about the history and culture of Estonia and how choral singing contributed to that history over hundreds of years. The readings also revealed a traditional, high regard for music in local churches.

Findings and Conclusions

Estonians migrated centuries ago from central Asia to their present location on the eastern shore of the Baltic Sea. Because of enduring German and Russian domination for centuries, Estonians feel they are not far removed from feudalism. In fact, feudalism was only abolished in the early nineteenth century. As a result, Estonians describe themselves as a singing, non-Western European peasant culture. This may seem a bit confusing, but Estonians are aware that their racial and linguistic heritage is distinctly Finno-Ugric, central Asian, and not Indo-European. They share this identity with Finns and Hungarians as well as some other smaller people groups.

Music, particularly singing, is such a strong ethnic symbol that it is virtually indistinguishable from the culture itself. Even before Christianity came to Estonian peasants, they were known to the outside world as a singing people. When the gospel first came to them through the Moravians during the 1730s, the message spread primarily through singing, not preaching. This interesting fact was previously verified by others who had researched letters sent to the Moravian headquarters in Herrnhut from missionaries in Estonia.

One scholar found that Estonians were so fond of singing during this period that punishment for offenses often included being barred from so-called "singing hours." His research also confirms the unusual musical ability of the peasants. One missionary wrote home, "For singing, they [Estonians] had much skill and could acquire the most difficult melodies" (Pöldmäe 1988, 68). This Christian singing movement eventually developed into a revival in the first part of the eighteenth century, which greatly contributed to the formation of the modern Estonian nation.

Through the gospel and the Enlightenment, through singing, and through a literacy movement inspired by the revival, Estonian peasants slowly began to realize and formulate their unique identity as a people. By the 1860s, a strong enough sense of this identity was present to organize the first Estonian national song festival. The German bureaucratic nobility and the Russian political classes were initially against such an expression of national fervor, but little could be done to prevent the event. The ethnic Estonians held their festival in the summer of 1869. Since then, the national song festival has been held twice each decade, even during the repressive days of the Soviet occupation.

While other peoples have similar song festivals, the Estonians' festivals constitute some of the largest—in proportion to the population—that the world has seen. In the summer of 1989, some observers estimated that nearly one-half the worldwide population of ethnic Estonians was present in Tallinn for the song festival.

During the Soviet period in Estonia, many traditional forms of ministry such as Christian literature and expository activities were severely limited. Pastors were very careful about their public statements, knowing that informers and representatives of Soviet internal security were always in attendance during meetings. However, choir activities were less restricted and, in many ways, singing fulfilled the function that we in Western Christianity usually associate exclusively with expository preaching and teaching. Churches featured high quality and large quantities of music. The people sang, and the act of singing kept Christianity alive and flourishing during a time when authorities deliberately attempted to abolish it.

It is important to point out that the function of singing did not emerge in response to the situation or the need. It had been present for centuries but rose to a level of even greater importance during the Soviet era.

When speaking specifically of Christian ministry, the interviews revealed a direct relationship between musical participation and Christian growth as they relate to revival, evangelism, personal experience, obedience to Scripture, learning theology, and youth work. Many people spoke freely about Christian music during the Soviet years and how it kept the church vital and growing during a very dark period. In addition, people also showed concern that changes are taking place in Estonian Christian music due to Western market-oriented influences. Still others felt free to speculate with considerable hope about the future of Estonian Christianity and Estonian Christian music.

During the interviews, many of the respondents expressed their strong commitment to the church and to the music of the church—making special note that singing, for them, was a life-changing ministry. As mentioned previously, most—including preachers—said they learned theology primarily through singing rather than preaching. Others said that insights into applications of Scripture came to them through singing. Virtually all said their personal relationship with the Lord was greatly enhanced and deepened through singing. One pastor summed it up by saying categorically that "singing is the first pulpit in Estonia; preaching is the second."

Another professional musician added, "We sang ourselves free, free from the Soviets, free from sin, free to serve the Lord." Indeed, in 1990, a "Singing Revolution" began at the song festival grounds. After a long period of corporate singing and political speeches, the Estonians took major political action that was to sever their bonds, within one year's time, with the Soviet Union. It should be noted that this political movement was completely peaceful. One researcher states that during this movement no one died or was even hospitalized as a result of violence (Taagepera 1993, 1). On September 18, 1991, Estonia had been recognized by the international community as a sovereign state and was accepted into the United Nations.

Thoughts on Missionary Training

As a missionary trained in North America, I found this information encouraging and, at the same time, disconcerting. Stumbling on a phenomenon that was so mightily used by the Lord over many years was a wonderful discovery. On the other hand, I realized from my own training and experience that Christian workers and missionaries educated in North America have been woefully under equipped to recognize and support such phenomena.

In general, pastors and missionaries have been trained with a Reformation emphasis that may be called "cognitive-linguistic." Their ministry centers on the verbal or written communication of cognitive-based concepts. In addition to our Reformation roots, the English-speaking world, in particular, exhibits an unusual emphasis on words and concepts, dating back to before the Elizabethan era. These patterns are so central to some pastors that they doubt they have truly "ministered" to others unless spiritual concepts have been communicated in specific and controlled linguistic ways. While few would argue the value of music, especially in worship, how many would be comfortable in allowing music to occupy the central position of ministry, as in the pattern found in Estonia?

As a result of these findings, I feel that Western missionary training should include artistic expression as a vital source for communicating the gospel and for Christian growth. This suggestion should not be interpreted that cognitive-linguistic training should in any way be restricted, but that it should be augmented to include artistic media. Few non-Westerners relate or respond to art in the manner we do in the broader North American culture where art in general and music in particular often fulfill an entertainment role. Our Western culture treats music mostly as a consumer item. As difficult as it is to admit, our churches often follow suit.

For many non-North Americans, art is much more central and vital to life and experience. Artistic expression can often communicate a truth with a richer emotional content, as well as implications and applications. In Estonia, Christians say they have not learned a truth fully until they have sung it, absorbing both its content and emotion in a manner that enables them to integrate it better into their daily lives.

What dedicated pastor would not be overjoyed at having such a powerful vehicle of communicating truth at his or her disposal? Many pastors and missionaries, however, are simply not equipped to recognize, let alone utilize, such a tool. In some cases, missionaries either consciously or unconsciously reject a host culture's artistic and musical traditions, sometimes even believing they are somehow intrinsically evil.

Missionaries, therefore, should be trained to research and identify the function of the arts in a host society in much the same way they are trained to recognize the function of other cultural phenomena. They may need to become familiar with the host culture's art forms by utilizing an assistant (much like a language assistant) to help decode and understand the symbolic language of the visual and performing arts as well as music. And, as in other matters of Western culture, missionaries should always be very careful about introducing Western Christian music or other art forms (either consciously or unconsciously) into host cultures. It would be far better to allow mature local Christians to develop their own hymnology and artistic language apart from Western influence, whenever possible.

Estonia has a deep and prophetic music culture. Many Estonian Christians are highly trained professional musicians who perform and compose at esteemed levels within the Estonian music culture. When the Soviet Union collapsed, many Western Christian groups sought to visit Eastern Europe to minister—with good intentions. However, their efforts often overwhelmed the people. Estonians began to view their culture as small and insignificant in light of powerful, well-organized, and highly financed Western Christian music groups.

From a musician's point of view, the situation appeared almost ridiculous. Untrained, often over-emotional, and technically limited, Western Christian musicians communicated either directly or indirectly to highly trained Estonian musicians that Western Christian music was somehow spiritually superior to Estonian Christian music, and by implication, it was suggested that changes were needed in Estonian music. The tragic part is that the message was heard and is being acted on in some circles, resulting in a change in Estonian Christian music to more generic commercial Western forms. Should the music that provided vital energy for Christian witness and growth during fifty years of repression disappear altogether, it would only be described as a deep human tragedy and a negation of a God-given gift. Happily, however, many Estonian Christian musicians are aware of the situation and are working to preserve their valuable heritage.

From my point of view, Westerners should visit other places primarily to listen and learn before attempting any ministry. Estonian Christians, as well as many others, have much to teach us. We as missionaries need always to be aware that the church of the living God is truly international. Our training can equip us to serve in a variety of ways cross-culturally, if we use sensitivity and common sense. We Westerners need to keep in mind that we need the perspective of the non-Western church and have much to learn from it. No one group of Christians has a corner on methods for communicating truth or on Christian practice. Scripture can be communicated and applied in a variety of ingenious and unexpected ways with respect to a people's history, context, and needs. Let us not impose a spiritual or even musical bondage on any people—especially the Estonians who sang themselves free!

References

Põldmäe, Rudolf. 1988. Vennaste-koguduse Muusikalisest Tegevusest Meie Maal. Translated by Margit Sepp. *Teater, Muusika, Kino* 3: 67–78.

Taagepera, Rein. 1993. *Estonia: Return to Independence*. Boulder, Colo.: Westview Press.

This article originally appeared in the *Evangelical Missions Quarterly*, 38:3 (2002). Used by permission.

Chapter 26

Northeast India

Ascending the Heights:
Glory to God in the Himalayas
by Frank Fortunato and Ken Davidson

Shortly before our plane started its descent, a flight attendant told us to look left. To our delight, we clearly saw the white peak of Mount Everest jutting above the clouds. Moments later we landed in West Bengal, high in the mountains of northern India and not far from the exotic city of Darjeeling, for what would be one of the most visually stunning and historically significant recording projects yet with Heart Sounds International (HSI).

In November 2005, we, Ken Davidson and Frank Fortunato, co-founders of HSI, were joined by Bob Eden, a Christian businessman from Georgia. Also on the team were Nancy Hudson, a church planter serving in South Africa, and her "spiritual son," Jonas Mangena, now pastor of a fast growing South African church. Our local coordinator was Dilip Dutt, an Indian church leader whose parents pioneered the India Evangelistic Crusade (IEC). The IEC had a remarkable beginning following a vision of the face of Jesus rising up out of the Himalayas and a voice saying, "I have many of my people hidden away in these mountains. Who will go to them?" Dilip's father and mother, newlyweds at the time, responded. That vision kept them strong through decades, resulting in 155 churches and 9,000 known believers, including nine orphanages and fifteen schools.

Our HSI project began when Nancy Hudson asked us to consider going to Calcutta to record the music of Dilip Dutt, an accomplished guitarist and songwriter. Dilip preferred, instead, to have HSI go into the mountains to record the unique worship songs sung in the IEC fellowship.

The day we landed, two rugged Indian Jeeps took our team of five and our precious cargo of digital audio and video recording equipment up the Himalayas to our first stop, the village of Tagdah, the location of the Joybells Orphanage.

Our first short night of sleep was shortened further by the orphan children's beautiful singing at 5:00 AM. We immediately discovered the monastic-like schedule of the orphanage, blessing the start and close of each day with times of worship. The children sang their Nepali dialect worship songs in near perfect unison, even when the songs were richly ornamented.

The church building on the orphanage grounds became a temporary recording studio with blankets and curtains providing sound insulation (typical for most HSI recording projects). When the recording sessions began, the children sang with abandon and ease, and the vocals were quickly captured, accompanied by simple drumming, guitar, and various local instruments.

The children then changed into their dance outfits, moved into the courtyard, and the audio team became a video team, taping several beautiful dances.

Besides the children, the HSI team also recorded some adult worship from the area. One of the IEC pastors, with a team of musicians, walked several hours to get to the orphanage for their recording session. Knowing that HSI was also videotaping, the team dressed in national dress for the recording session.

Following the visit to Tagdah, Bob and I went to the Operation Mobilization India headquarters in Hyderabad to make preparations for future HSI recordings for Dalit (former "untouchables") children who are being educated in fifty Dalit Education Centers run by Operation Mobilization India.

Meanwhile, the recording team moved to other parts of northeastern India, recording various people groups associated with the IEC. In nearly every place, locals welcomed the team into the village by dance and procession, and then by foot washing and water sprinkling—rituals of the area.

One of the recording sessions included the Oraon people who have African origins. Pastor Jonas was deeply moved as his common heritage was expressed in their drumming, dance, and singing. He also had the joy of leading seventeen people to make spiritual commitments at one of the meetings.

The team then journeyed several hours into a remote part of the Himalayas to visit the Lepchas, original inhabitants of this part of India. Some novel moments of audio and video were captured as the believers, using handmade stringed and rhythm instruments, worshiped and danced, surrounded by the majestic beauty of the mountains and valleys.

Next, the HSI team traveled through the forest on acutely forbidding roads to the northeastern Indian state of Assam, a place that had experienced much hardship and oppression over many decades. People stared curiously as they saw their first black African and their first white missionaries. In at least three remote villages, the team comprised the first foreigners ever to visit there.

Over several days Ken and the team captured Christian villagers rejoicing in the Lord through their native song and dance. The suffering and difficulties experienced by these people have produced deep expressions of total abandonment in worship to the God who has become their life and sustenance.

The final people visited were the Totos, also located in a remote region in close proximity to the country of Bhutan. At the time they were oppressively cast out of that country, the Totos were killed, almost to extinction. They now number about 1,200, after having diminished to a low of 460. We were honored to meet several of the new believers and were able to record a couple of their recently composed worship songs.

Because the team was working in such remote parts with no electricity, Ken boldly experimented with capturing audio through sophisticated laptop and digital accessories, all running on computer battery or external battery units. In turn, these needed recharging through the night. Also, we were ready to use the Jeep battery, if necessary. Amazingly, enough juice flowed in the high-tech equipment to record the tracks without a hitch!

In all, the team recorded twenty-four tracks in nine dialects, including Nepali, Talmang, Lepcha, Oraon, Rabha, Santhal, Bodo, Assamese, and Toto. It was significant that the Himalaya project included both audio and video, as each group provided authentic, ancient forms of music and dance, complete in their natural mountain environment.

As we departed the Himalayas, towering Mount Everest stunned us yet again in all its awesome majesty—the backdrop in understanding what we had just experienced. We had been privileged to uncover a mostly hidden part of the planet where people not only have learned to live in the mountain heights, but have also learned to express humble, abandoned worship that ascends to the heavenlies. From the high mountain ranges of the earth God has indeed raised up heights of global praise.

Following these recordings, the HSI engineer mixed all the tracks—over several months and in his spare time—and discussed with the leader from India ways to distribute the recorded songs. As is customary, HSI sent the final mixed recorded copy back to the country, with definite plans to encourage the local leadership to distribute the new music as widely as possible.

Chapter 27

Northeast India

Touched by Jesus:
The Dalit Music Seminar
Author Unknown

Millions of Dalits* across India are embracing new belief systems, seeking the freedom—socially and religiously—denied them for centuries. A large group have chosen Jesus as the Truth and the Way to ultimate release. As a result, thousands of new Dalit believers hunger for discipleship. They want to grow in their knowledge of God. They want to pray. They want to worship. They want to experience Jesus Christ personally. It is Operation Mobilization (OM) India's goal to help Dalits know the living God and enjoy every aspect of their new-found faith.

Part of authentic Christian worship is music. OM India wants to help new believers develop a style of worship uniquely their own. Workers feel Dalits deserve fully indigenous songs to express their adoration of Jesus. To help them achieve this blessing, in late October 2003, OM personnel in northern India held a first-ever event to initiate the development of Dalit worship music.

The Dalit Music Seminar had a four-fold purpose. First, OM India wanted to identify local Dalit singers, lyricists, and musicians. Second, event organizers wanted these musicians to perform their own traditional songs in their own musical style. Third, in order to inspire them to write new Dalit worship songs, they decided to give the musicians a copy of the New Testament in their own language and show them the *Dayasagar* film (the life of Christ filmed in an Indian context). Finally, OM India purposed to explore the possibility of producing a worship album for use in the Dalit community in India.

The two-day event proved a complete success. Eighteen musicians from the region gathered together. OM India's workers began the event by singing *bhajans* (traditional Indian worship songs, now with Christian lyrics) and Christian folk songs. Then, the OM North India field leader, Moses Parmar, taught a Bible lesson about the woman who washed Jesus' feet with perfume. Dalit participants commented that they understood this story well because, like the woman in the story, they know what it is to be rejected by some and accepted by others. Dalit musicians then sang a few of their own songs, commending both Dr. B. R. Ambedkar (a Dalit, and father of the Indian constitution) and Jesus—both who readily accepted people who were sinful or rejected by society.

OM India workers learned that both the theme and style of Dalit music reflect the Dalit situation and speak to the rural non-literate or semi-literate Dalit person. The rhythm of each song is captivating and easy to learn. Musicians sing songs that clearly narrate stories, explaining the intended message. The lead singer sings a line and the choir or audience repeats it. They also use a "heckler," a member of the singing group. He poses arguments or questions about the song's story that audience members may be afraid to ask. The lead singer clearly answers the heckler's questions through sung illustrations or short stories, even as the audience continues to repeat the refrain.

During the music seminar, Dalit musicians were able to write new songs quickly after learning new stories from the Bible or new concepts about the character of God. Their songs traditionally contain tributes to men, women, and leaders who had either enlightened them or fought for their rights. Today, musicians are keen to add Jesus Christ to that list. New songs are being produced that include a message of hope: that Christ and his teachings can be the liberation for which the Dalits have been searching.

The music seminar was an exciting event, yet it is just the beginning of a long process to help Dalits worship in their own heart language and style. OM India workers plan to hold more seminars in the future. They are also working toward producing both a Dalit worship album and a Dalit worship song book.

The transformation of the Dalit people—physical, social, and spiritual—is well underway. They are discovering that Jesus is not only the Way and the Truth, but also the Life they have long sought for and now found.

*Dalits were formerly called "untouchables."

This article is adapted from its first edition in *Operation Mobilization India News*, 2, 2004.

Movement 3:
Church
Strengthening

Chapter 28

Mali

Body, Soul, and Spirit:
Malian Evangelicals Worship to the Beat of Their Hearts
by Phil Anderson

Music has always played an important role in the social and religious life of the Malian people. In a country where most people are not literate, oral communication is essential, and singing especially is woven into the very heart of Malian culture. Every joyous occasion is celebrated with music. Every rite of passage has its songs. Marriage, tribal rituals, death, oncoming danger, victory in battle, or the worship of idols—each event has its message in music and rhythm. The Malian woman sings her joy or her frustration as she pounds grain. The men in the fields chant their encouragement to each other, sometimes to the beat of a drummer, as they hoe their crops.

Music is also a medium for communicating the mores of Malian society. Songs arrest the people's attention and drive home a message that can't be communicated adequately by plain verbal exchange or counsel. Malians may accept a message in song regarding the virtues of hard work, honesty, and faithfulness, but pay no attention to the same message espoused by a preacher.

The first contact Malians had with Christian music was with Western hymns. Missionaries of the 1930s and '40s took favorites from English and French and translated them into the Bambara language. In most cases the music came along with the translation, although there were exceptions. "Auld Lang Syne" and "The Old Gray Goose Is Dead" went through a transformation and became sanctified with new words to an old tune.

This new music was foreign to the ears of Malians, the rhythms occidental and staid. They accepted it without question, however, for it was considered to be a part of the new road they were walking. They desired to sing the glories of their new deity.

Accustomed to maintaining oral traditions, Malian Christians easily memorized the Christian lyrics and soon claimed the music as their own. They broke out spontaneously into song, often changing the tunes to fit their five-note scale. A few pastors and laypeople began writing songs that were also used in worship services. But something was still missing, for when Africans express themselves, they want to do it with their whole being: body, soul, and spirit. Handclapping, drums, and some other instruments had been frowned upon by missionaries and older believers who considered them part of the old life. Changes came slowly, but the church's music steadily became more Malian.

One of the greatest encouragements Gospel Missionary Union* missionaries gave the Bambara church was to print, bind, and distribute its songs almost as fast as they were written. Well over six hundred original songs and choruses have now been published in books. Many more are passed on orally, bringing the actual number of Christian songs written by Malians to more than one thousand. Some songs have their genesis in other language groups and find their way across the country, going through one translation after another. The old hymnal of translated songs from English and French is still the "King James Version" to some. But when it comes to singing for enjoyment, it's their own songs and melodies that Bambara Christians turn to.

Today, new forms are emerging from the old. The ever-present *griot* (singing storyteller) at most social events is a tradition for Malians. They have always loved his music, and now a Christian griot is beginning to share the good news in this ancient form. Choreography and body language are becoming more important as church music is "Malianized."

Drums and other rhythm instruments as well as handclapping are commonplace. West African instruments like the *balaphone* (similar to the xylophone), the 22-stringed *kora,* and the guitar-like *ngoni* are being introduced here and there, along with electronic instruments in the cities. As global communications bring the rest of the world closer, it is not unusual to hear music in Malian churches that reflects the influence of American country, soul, or reggae.

It is interesting to see the influence the church has had on other religious groups within Mali. There was a time when Christian music was criticized, but now it is being copied as the leaders of other religions look for ways to keep their people from coveting the joyful worship of the evangelicals. Music is the common ground for non-literates and intellectuals, believers and unbelievers. With the coming of dozens of FM radio stations and the increased availability of television, the influence of Christian music in Mali is growing. More attention is being paid to ensure that the message is true to Scripture and to maximize its impact.

A Bambara proverb says, "The tune is bad, but the meaning of the words is very pleasing." The music of the Malian church will never hit the charts in North America or Europe, but it is reaching the ears and hearts of Malians because it is theirs.

*Gospel Missionary Union is now called Avant Ministries.

This article originally appeared in *The Gospel Message,* 1999:3, pp. 2–3.

Chapter 29

Tanzania

"From Now On, Give Us This Bread"
by Julie Taylor

"We had no idea the church could be like this!" said two elderly ladies from Tanzania, drawn to Christ through the music of their own culture.

They had come to a May 2004 indigenous hymnody workshop among the Burunge people. Knowing older people are often the last guardians of local cultural practices, I had invited several to the church where the workshop was held.

Seven traditional ladies came, but they refused to speak Kiswahili, the national language of Tanzania, which is also used in churches. They were proud of their mother tongue, Burunge, and insisted on using it. These ladies had seldom crossed the threshold of a church because the language and music used in the services was alien to them. Nevertheless, at the end of the song workshop, having spent a week combining Scripture texts in their own language with their own music styles, two of them gave their lives to the Lord.

Many people in eastern Africa worship God with music styles they cannot identify with, understand, or even enjoy. "This is the way it has always been," they say. "We sing these hymns because that is what we were taught."

Physical drought has existed so long in parts of eastern Africa that many children don't even know what bread is. Another kind of drought has hindered indigenous music from flourishing.

In some areas, indigenous music styles have been almost completely abandoned in exchange for more modern, foreign, or "correct" styles. Younger generations no longer identify with or have any experience in singing songs from their own culture.

At the same time, hunger for better understanding of God's Word persists, and one of the fastest ways to satisfy that craving is through music. We want to help meet that hunger through these indigenous hymnody workshops.

The ladies who attended the classes brought an instrument with them that I had never seen before—a friction trough (*khuu'usimoo*). Laid on the ground with women players sitting at both ends, each simultaneously rubbed two large wooden "spoons" on the convex board to produce a series of pitched "grunts," not unlike a fire-making technique. I was so excited I could hardly speak. This highly revered instrument, traditionally reserved for secret female-only ceremonies, now was used—in the open—to praise God in a musical setting of Psalm 23.

As the women began to play the instrument, and others began to sing and dance, men at the workshop fell respectfully silent, listening intently to the new words. No one was confused by the message or by the outward style—the "clothing"—of the song. It obviously felt entirely natural; the song belonged to the Burunge people, based on the culture God had given them.

In John 6:33–35, Jesus said,

> "For the bread of God is he who comes down from heaven and
> gives life to the world."
> "Sir," they said, "from now on give us this bread."
> Then Jesus declared, "I am the bread of life. He who comes to
> me will never go hungry, and he who believes in me will never
> be thirsty."

The drought of culturally-appropriate Christian music is ending for the Burunge people as the Bread of Life comes and satisfies them—body, soul, and spirit.

This article is adapted from Dr. Taylor's newsletter article "Give Us this Bread," which was published in *EthnoDoxology*, February–March 2004.

Chapter 30

Bolivia

Singing a New Song:
How Music Came to the Guaraní
by Jeanette Windle

If only they had an accordion of their own. They had written the song in their native Guaraní and had practiced diligently. But the guitar was an old one, the accordion borrowed and battered and so small it could almost have been a child's plaything. And never before had any group from the Güirapembi church ever competed in the great music festival.

Juan Segundo looked out across the restless crowd gathered under the vast tarp—two thousand at least, each with the eyes and ears of a critic. He nodded to his band of young musicians.

> Tumpa ometa ndeve
> Iporoaiu añete vae
> Jae oyangareko
> Metei ñavo re.
> (God give you
> The love that is true;
> He cares for each one.)

The interweaving of guitar and accordion and solemn male voices faded, only to be swallowed up by a thunder of applause. The applause was even more thunderous when the winners of the 1998 Annual Guaraní

Christian Music Festival were announced. First place went to the small band from Güirapembi. The prize: an accordion.

The Exception

A year earlier, no one would have predicted that a group of young men from Güirapembi would be standing on the music festival's outdoor "stage"—a cordoned-off section of sandy soil—much less carrying home first prize.

The Guaraní, Bolivia's largest lowland tribe, had experienced one of the earliest and most sweeping movements of God in Bolivian church history. Mid-century, whole villages turned to Christ, and churches sprang up across Guaraní territory. Recent decades had seen some stagnation of that earlier growth. A contributing factor was the shortage of pastors or lay leaders with training in the Scriptures. There were, too, the constant attacks of foreign anthropologists who, in the name of preserving Guaraní culture, spent large sums to push the tribe back into its traditional spirit worship, devil dancing, and drunken festivals. Still, a full 60 percent of the inhabitants of Isoso, the semi-arid region where some of the first Guaraní churches were established, identified themselves as evangelical Christians.

Güirapembi was an exception. It was the *curandero*, the witch doctor, who ruled like a king there. The people of the community scurried to tend his fields, carry his water, satisfy his every demand. There had been a church once, but the members had drifted away. Its adobe walls were broken down, the thatched roof caved in.

When Juan Segundo, a well-known Guaraní lay leader, accepted in early 1997 the challenge of pastoring the Güirapembi church, he faced tremendous opposition from the curandero and the community. The work was brutal: toiling in the fields all day to feed his family, walking long distances in the evenings to visit homes. But one by one, individuals and entire families accepted Christ. As the small body of believers grew, they rebuilt the crumbling walls of the church and repaired the roof. A talented musician, Juan started a music group among the young people. The church had no instruments of its own, but the people began to put aside a few bolivianos. Maybe someday they would have enough money to buy an accordion.

Now, a year after his arrival in Güirapembi, Juan was seeing the fruits of his labor—not so much in the firstplace finish at the music contest as in the faith of the young men receiving the crowd's acclaim. As for the prize, it was as though God himself had reached down from heaven to whisper how much he cared for them. They would no longer have to borrow to practice. Their little church would have music of its own.

Seeds of Christian Songs

In light of these developments, it is surprising to realize that in Guaraní culture, instrumental music never existed and vocal music had a different basis than western music. The village cantor would assist the curandero with a series of sacred chants—powerful but purposefully unintelligible.

Nevertheless, the Guaraní had been apt pupils of Christian song taught by Spanish Roman Catholic missionaries since the 16th century. It wasn't until the first Protestant missionaries arrived in the late 1920s that the Guaraní were widely introduced to the western concept of popular song. The oldest believers still remember early open-air meetings with Bible messages in Guaraní and lively Spanish choruses—as unintelligible to most as the cantor's chants!

The missionaries quickly learned the Guaraní language and began translating Spanish choruses and English church hymns into Guaraní. In the early '40s, Gospel Missionary Union* (GMU) pioneer Leslie Harwood published the first Guaraní hymnbook, containing more than two hundred songs. The Guaraní Christians grew to enjoy congregational singing. After all, the book of God the missionaries had brought said much about making a joyful noise to the Lord.

Still, their church music continued to be translated from foreign languages and cultures. And it wasn't until 1966, when two young Guaraní men returned to Isoso after some time with a music group in Argentina, that the concept of performing for an audience was introduced. Organizing youth choirs in two of the main churches, the men began showing up with special music at regional Bible conferences. The Guaraní had no native instruments, but they borrowed the guitar from the Spanish and the accordion from the missionaries. Innovative percussion instruments—a stick rubbed across a grooved log or a plastic paint bucket with rawhide stretched across the top—contributed rhythms that were uniquely their own. In 1974, the first Guaraní music festival was organized, offering some original compositions as well as translated music. The festivals continued annually until 1981, when the Guaraní churches, in a period of stagnation, lost interest.

Worth the Effort

In 1994, missionaries Curtis Juett and David Turner arrived in Bolivia to work with GMU's new radio studio, Life Recordings. An early goal was to produce a daily Guaraní radio program. Teachers were found for the program, but the missionaries were disappointed to discover that only four music cassettes existed in Guaraní, the most recent being ten years old.

Nor did a visit to Isoso improve the situation. There were few music groups and no music of high enough quality to record.

The older Guaraní believers remembered the music festivals of the 1970s. Why not start them again? So in the fall of 1995, in conjunction with a regional youth conference, Life Recordings sponsored the first Guaraní music festival in fourteen years.

It was a disappointment. Only four music groups showed up, and the whole program was over in a half-hour. But the winner received a guitar, and the missionaries returned home with a few new songs for the radio program. As the churches saw that a real prize was forthcoming and that the sponsors were serious about putting their music on the air, enthusiasm mounted. Eight groups showed up at the next festival, just a few months later during the Carnival holiday of 1996. In 1997, there were eleven groups. By 1998, fourteen groups were performing with more than two thousand in attendance, and an accordion was added as first prize. Eighteen groups participated in the 1999 competition.

Festival rules are simple. All music must be in Guaraní with strong Christian content. Music must be written entirely by the contestants or arranged from traditional hymns. Instruments must be non-electronic.

The language requirement is a problem for young people who grow up speaking Guaraní but are taught to read and write mainly in Spanish. They are not used to forming rhymes in their own language. And only this year is translation being finished on the Guaraní Old Testament, with its wealth of imagery and poetry that has inspired so much Christian music in other languages.

"One of the difficulties we're having," Curtis Juett says, "is a lack of depth or complexity in the lyrics. The Guaraní youth complain that they don't know how to write songs in Guaraní."

Is it worth the effort, then, to promote Guaraní Christian music when so much of the tribe now understands at least minimal Spanish? You have only to see the enthusiasm of the festivals, the joy on the faces of Guaraní Christians when they sing in their heart language, the excitement when their own music is aired on the radio, to know that it is.

Tumpa Cheparavo Ma

Tumpa cheparavo ma
God chose me

Jae cheraiu ramo
He loves me, oh, so much

Jae chembori öi
He gives me his help

Yembori ara igua ndie
The help that comes from heaven

Kuae ko Tumpa oyapo
All of this God did

Ndei ivi oiko mbove
Before the creation of the world

Jae jemimbota rupi
It is his will I see

Cheparavo ma
That he has chosen me for his own

And the music festivals are making a difference. This year 80 percent of the contestants presented original songs written in Guaraní, and the quality of both lyrics and music is improving. Within the next year, the first complete Guaraní Bible will be released, and plans are underway for a festival of music written entirely from Bible passages. Another Guaraní settlement, Heití, an area much less evangelized than Isoso, has requested a music festival of its own. And the Guaraní churches are making plans for ministry teams to carry their music and the gospel to unreached communities.

So the church grows stronger as a new generation of Guaraní Christians takes pen, guitar, and accordion in hand to raise a joyful sound to the Lord.

*Gospel Missionary Union is now called Avant Ministries.

This article is slightly revised from the original which appeared in *The Gospel Message*, 1999:3, pp. 6–9, 11.

Chapter 31

Brazil

Now We Can Speak to God—in Song
by Jack Popjes

We were stumped. The musical system of the Canela people of Brazil's Amazon jungle had us completely baffled. Not because my wife Jo and I were tone deaf or didn't appreciate music—we sang for years in many musical groups. Not because we never heard Canela music. We were constantly surrounded by it while in the village. Every night the Canela sang us to sleep with their massive sing-songs at the village's central plaza.

We tried to learn to sing Canela, but we just couldn't. We could not make head nor tail either of the rhythm or the tone system. Whenever we joined their singing and dancing, Jo didn't know what to sing, and I didn't know when to stomp my feet. How could we ever promote the composition of native Canela hymns when, even after nearly twenty years of praying and trying, we just couldn't get the hang of their music?

Enter Tom Avery, a Wycliffe ethnomusicology consultant. Tom taped Canela music for several weeks. He took the music to his study and analyzed it, using a computer. The next year we got together, and he introduced me to the rudiments of Canela music—at last.

Differences

Now we knew why we had never been able to learn it. Instead of a musical system of eight notes with some half notes, the Canela system has many more notes. Although Canela music can be sung or played on an instrument such as a violin or a slide flute, it is impossible to play on a keyboard.

Another difference was the words. So many additional syllables and fillers are put on the basic words, it was almost impossible to understand the lyrics. I guess we do something a bit like that with some of our songs. Think of "Glo-o-o-o-o-ria" in the Christmas carol with each "o" on a different note and beat, or "fa la la la" fillers in another carol.

The Canela system was not simple. Just as a symphony has distinct parts like the overture, so the Canela music system has three main types. At every major or minor songfest, they always start with the slow, walking-style *ihkenpoc* songs. Then they move to the faster jogging-style *kyjkyj* music and end up with a full cry, racing *ihkenpej* music. Tom discovered all this and more. Then he came back to us. As I provided Scripture-based lyrics, Tom composed original Canela music for more than twenty hymns.

Great Acceptance

We traveled to the Canela village to introduce the songs to the people. It was almost like pouring gasoline on a campfire! Within a few nights, hundreds of Canelas crowded around wanting to listen and to learn the new songs. The main song and dance leader was deeply moved. He wanted a hymnbook for himself and sat for hours listening to a tape we had prepared. He eventually learned all the songs and made improvements on them. Other Canelas started adding verses to some of the hymns.

Every night during our evening Bible classes with the Canela, more than half of the time was taken up singing the new songs. One Canela, with tears in his eyes, said, "You gave us the book in which God speaks to us, but your friend Tom gave us songs in which we speak to him."

After the dedication of the Scriptures in 1990, all the Canela men and women who had received their copy of God's translated Word crowded around the main song leader in the center of the plaza. They sang several of the Canela songs, such as "God's Word Is Sweeter Than Honey to Me" and "Let Us Hold on to and Obey God's Word."

Tom's culturally sensitive work sped up not only the acceptance of the newly translated Scriptures, but also the whole gospel message among the Canela.

The original title of this article is "Music to Their Ears: An Ethnomusicologist Helps the Canelas of Brazil Worship More Meaningfully."

Chapter 32

Kenya

Music Worth Celebrating
by James Ziersch

We sat on cold metal chairs in the near-empty town hall anxiously waiting, while myriads of questions flew through our minds. *How many people will come to a new event such as this? Will all the official guests arrive? Will people appreciate the displays? Will there be enough seats? Do we have too many seats? Have we overplanned?*

After spending two months in preparation for a Marakwet* Language and Culture Day, now all was ready. Posters announced the big day. In one meeting after another we had fine-tuned events. Numerous phone calls and visits ensured our special guests would come.

May 7 would be a day for the Marakwet of Kenya to celebrate their own language and culture. Most important, it would mark the efforts of the partnership since 1983 between Bible Translation and Literacy (BTL) and the Marakwet: translation and literacy work accomplished by the Marakwet and missionaries alike.

As an opportunity to *glorify* God and show his hand in what had been achieved, this needed to be a full-blown celebration. We decided against the usual village church venue that many Marakwet had come to expect. Instead, we chose the town hall of their nearest, main town. Our aim: an event that would be more spectacular than a few special guests seated at a long table on an otherwise empty stage.

Nearly one hundred photographs of Marakwet places, events, and history, accompanied by cultural artifacts, would complement the program. A careful historical outline of the language project and a display of BTL booklets and Scripture portions would give proof of what was already translated and published.

An aged man had also been invited to play music on his *pukan*, a special stringed instrument once played regularly among the Marakwet.

Yet most important, several weeks before in a workshop led by SIL ethnomusicologist Dr. Julie Taylor, twenty-eight Marakwet musicians composed several songs especially for this celebration. The workshop had ended on an unexpected high note. Kenya's president happened to come to town for a speech, and Julie persuaded organizers to allow her students to perform three new songs for him. "They did wonderfully well," she said. "It was an honor to the president, and good publicity for Bible translation."

This newly-created Cultural Composer's Choir would perform several cultural songs, giving the celebration an unmistakably Marakwet flavor. The music would be truly Marakwet with the words of the songs coming straight from the translated Marakwet Scriptures.

With only moments to go, we sat and wondered how the day's events would unfold.

Praise God, we were not disappointed.

The local government minister surprised us by arriving early. Marakwet people trailed into the town hall, slowly at first, but later, in droves. The government representative for sports and culture was enthralled and excited by the various displays.

Most encouraging was the Composer Choir's opening performance. Once the combined rhythm of feet and voices resounded beyond the hall, curious faces began to appear at the doorway. One after another, they came into the hall until it was filled with an excited, curious audience. Captured by sounds and rhythms, new yet strangely familiar, people stood motionless and listened. It was a music from the past, but used little for generations, often due to early missions with misguided intentions, portraying cultural music as bad, even evil.

As we saw the growing sense of recognition coming across faces, we knew God had truly inspired, redeemed, and blessed this music for his glory. We also realized that this cultural, Christian music could indeed be a key for literacy and mother-tongue scriptural music throughout the Marakwet church.

Our thoughts were confirmed as we watched the government minister, a Marakwet, pull back her chair and join the choir in singing and dancing before an enthralled audience. That was a sign for others to follow. One after another, each special guest joined the singing and dancing in child-like abandonment. Whoops of joy and clapping from the audience signaled their appreciation as the dancing continued unabated. What was to have been a seven-minute introduction turned into a fifteen-minute spectacle. Finally, people began to slowly return to their seats with smiles of satisfaction and joy. This opening event assured everyone that the Marakwet could indeed praise God in their own language, using a truly cultural mode and style.

As the program unfolded, event after event, speech after speech, all attested to a growing awareness: yes, the Marakwet do indeed have a history and culture worth celebrating. Pride in one's language and culture, so often an essential element in progressing politically, socially, and economically, was here, alive and well. Now, during this special celebration, many saw their culture and language elevated in ways they had never thought possible.

The following day at a village church service, the congregation began singing a song in Swahili, the Kenyan trade language. The Marakwet government minister stopped the congregation halfway through, saying, "Please, can we stop this. The songs I heard on Saturday, where are they? That's what I want to hear."

Someone who had been at the Language and Culture Day then led the congregation in cultural Christian songs, followed by loud applause.

On hearing this, our anxious concern for the success of this day turned into jubilant praise, praise to our God who created every language and uses each one to speak to hearts—especially through the wonderful medium of mother-tongue song.

*Though not yet formally recorded, the name of this project was changed in July 2005 from Endo to Marakwet so as to incorporate all Marakwet speakers, not just the Endo, a clan grouping and part of the wider Marakwet speaking language.

Chapter 33

Cameroon

Let's Worship—in Ejagham!
Author Unknown

"When I preach, young people want me to use English; older people want to hear their own language, Ejagham. But when it comes to singing, *everyone* loves songs in Ejagham. I know this because I hear young people, and old, going to and from their farms singing Ejagham worship songs. In the past, they never sang songs in English like that."

Encouraging Ejagham language use in church was the focus at a pastors' conference held in 2001 in a remote corner of southwest Cameroon. Twenty pastors and church leaders gathered from many denominations in the Ejagham language area. Baptist, Catholic, Deeper Life Bible, Full Gospel, Presbyterian, and Apostolic churches sent representatives. All were unified for two days while they discussed the use of the Ejagham New Testament and of Ejagham as a language for ministry in their churches.

A new Ejagham songbook was a hit; so much so, that organizers worked hard to convince the representatives to stop learning and singing Ejagham Scripture songs and move on to other topics! One participant recounted how people in his church responded to singing Ejagham Scripture songs: "If we do what these songs say, our lives will go better."

By the end of the conference, some pastors testified and even more pastors came to realize that using Ejagham in worship services changes church attendance, attitudes, and lives.

The impact of the conference continues. At a recent funeral for an Ejagham believer, a popular youth choir led the celebration of the man's life. They sang Scripture-based songs set to Ejagham tunes adapted to modern-day instruments (guitar rather than traditional drums). God's Word brought comfort to all who heard it through song.

As the pastors discovered, songs touch the hearts of all ages. No wonder they say, "Let's worship in our own language—in Ejagham!"

The Ejagham language of southwest Cameroon and southeast Nigeria has 120,000 speakers. The New Testament was dedicated in December 1997. Tom and Eileen Edmondson and John and Kathie Watters with Wycliffe Bible Translators, and Ayamba Nkiri with the Cameroon Association for Bible Translation and Literacy (CABTAL), a partner organization in Cameroon, have been involved in the project, assisted by Ejagham pastors.

Chapter 34

Ghana

"Now There's Something Interesting in Church!"
by Leticia Dzokotoe

"An old woman, a church member, died. At the funeral, non-Christian relatives performed traditional funeral rites. Then they said, 'Now it's the Christians' turn.' Most of the townspeople started to leave, thinking nothing interesting would happen. As they walked away, church members started singing—not just any song, but new, indigenous Christian songs with traditional drumming. People turned on their heels and started running back from all directions. Some grabbed branches to wave as they danced, declaring, 'Now there's something interesting in church!'"*

Not only did the indigenous hymns call people back to the funeral, they also drew more to church services in the weeks that followed. Previously, the church had used translated hymns and choruses from other languages that did not reflect the Bassari musical system. Now, church music is no longer considered boring, foreign, or irrelevant. The church uses Bassari music for Bassari people, and everyone wants to listen.

All this was the fruit of a hymn workshop in which participants had composed new Christian songs in a musical genre that was falling into disuse. This revitalized the genre and gave new life to traditional music at the same time that it effectively proclaimed the gift and excitement of new life in Christ.

*From a report by Pastor Emmanuel Nambu of Ghana, West Africa, on the power of new songs created at a Scripture Use Workshop for the Bassari people in the village of Kpandai.

Movement 4:
Culture Affirmation

Chapter 35

Mongolia

Cresting a Musical Wave
by Frank Fortunato and Paul Neeley

We were invaded—suddenly and unexpectedly by God's presence. His Spirit rode in on the crest of the song.

Two steel shipping containers welded together, wired, paneled, and outfitted for recording had become far more than a tiny, makeshift studio in Ulan Bator, Mongolia. As we started recording the first song by a young team of Mongolian worship musicians, God pressed into the room, creating a sacred moment as we experienced his power. Indeed, we worshiped in a miniature, God-saturated, steel-clad cathedral. What an exhilarating start to our second Heart Sounds International (HSI) visit to Mongolia!

The opportunity to record this worship team from Erdenet, Mongolia's third largest city, traced back to our songwriting workshop held sixteen months earlier in 2002. Buynaa, one of the worship leaders, had asked us then to consider recording worship music from her church. Included in the songs we recorded on this visit was one she had composed the previous year.

Having only six days to do a multi-track recording of eleven Mongolian worship songs stretched us all. Despite the pressure, we noticed over and over how the team maintained a sincere and intense love for Jesus and for each other. Surely, the memorable times of intercession we shared most mornings prepared us for the rigorous schedule.

The beautiful depth of the song lyrics was supported by a high quality of musicianship, both in composition and performance. For one of the songs, Ganaa, the keyboardist and main songwriter for the group, recorded a solo. She approached the microphone timidly, asking us to pray. A few seconds later, Ken and I were stunned as Ganaa sang with the intensity, nuance, vocal control, and passion of a seasoned, professional recording artist.

The day-long recording sessions were only a small part of what happened during our two-week Mongolia visit. While Ken Davidson and I, Frank Fortunato, leaders of HSI, worked on recording the Erdenet worship songs, other members of the HSI team led a workshop each evening for both traditional and contemporary songwriting. About twenty-five local people participated. Composers with a focus on traditional music created Christian songs in existing musical genres that utilized the pentatonic (five-note) scale prevalent in this part of the world. Many of these songs utilized plucked Asian instruments, as well as flutes and hammered dulcimers, which have been used for centuries.

In addition, several composers at the evening workshop sessions wrote songs in contemporary western styles. Western classical and pop styles have been embedded in Mongolian culture through decades of Russian influence. Western pop sounds dominate the youth culture as well as the worship services in the young Mongolian churches.

Because of our vision to promote indigenous approaches to worship, HSI launched a third activity in Mongolia: an internship program. Paul Neeley, one of the HSI leaders with an ethnomusicology focus, mentored Erica Logan. On assignment with the Music in World Cultures graduate ethnomusicology program at Bethel College in Minneapolis, Erica conducted interviews with people in the city. A major focus was getting feedback on the various types of songs (using traditional and contemporary music styles) composed the previous year. It was gratifying that a number of people reacted positively to the use of Christian lyrics with some traditional song forms. This research will guide HSI and local worship leaders in deciding what contextualized Christian song forms might be most popular among certain sub-groups of the population, including nomadic herders.

In the previous year's visit, as well as this one in 2003, the Lord unexpectedly brought a prominent Mongolian musician-composer (who is also a pastor) to take a leadership role in the events. This year, Pastor Puje came into our network through a Filipino Operation Mobilization leader overseeing events in Mongolia.

Pastor Puje had found Christ at the first church planted in Mongolia when the country opened its doors to evangelism. During the week of song writing, he shared his dream to create a Christian songwriting fellowship, as well as an annual music concert to celebrate new songs birthed each year. The HSI team immediately started praying and working behind the scenes to encourage the formation of a music and worship committee. With very little persuasion, Pastor Puje agreed to lead it.

As in the previous year's trip, the crowning event of our visit was a music concert featuring the new songs composed at the workshop. A standing-room-only crowd squeezed into the small church hall to witness the two-part concert. More than an hour's worth of indigenous songs and poetry with Christian themes dominated the first part. The second part featured new, contemporary Christian songs driven by guitar or keyboard.

One highlight of the evening was the very first public presentation of Christian Mongolian children's songs. Nearly a dozen songs had been written by members of the newly formed songwriters fellowship. Previously, only three such original—not translated—children's songs were known in the country, all composed by Pastor Puje.

As we recorded songs (about forty during our fifteen-day stay) and discussed CD and cassette distribution, God showed us ways we could partner with Mongolian churches and expatriate missionaries to reach the entire 250 churches in the nation with indigenous Christian music. This would also include starting an underground movement to begin reaching believers in the house churches among the four million people living in Inner Mongolia (a part of China). Through prayer, networking, and brainstorming, preliminary plans were presented in a multi-year proposal.

Looking back, the entire visit was clearly orchestrated by the Lord—even though we had arrived with a sense of dismay and uncertainty. Through months of endless emails and phone calls, we had requested particular preparations and planning. But when our six-member HSI team arrived in the country, we found few preparations had been made. However, by the end of our visit, we sensed God had unfolded a plan that was far greater than our human efforts. He had prepared something hugely significant for the worship life of the whole nation. As he moved quickly in many areas of church life, we breathlessly tried to keep up with it all.

While sharing thoughts about this among ourselves, quiet team member Erica smiled and said, "I was wondering how long it would take the team to finally figure this out." She then added that weeks before she had joined the team, God had spoken to several of her friends about the trip, in particular a prayer warrior. God had shown her that Erica and her team members would have a small part in something God was birthing across the entire nation. She also shared several Scriptures with Erica that confirmed this prophetic word.

We then understood why we had been so invigorated day after day. It gradually dawned on us that during our short visit, we had been small instruments in a great symphony God was already orchestrating across this land. God had not only anointed those early moments of the first song we recorded, but he had also empowered the entire visit. We were merely swept along, riding the crest of a musical wave inundating what many no longer see as a spiritually landlocked country—Mongolia.

Chapter 36

Mongolia

Artistic Expression Offered as Worship:
God at Work in Mongolia
by Frank Fortunato
with Paul and Linda Neeley

As I opened a newly printed songbook destined for Inner Mongolia, my thumb "just happened" to land on song number 102. Starting to hum the very ornate melody, I realized, to my astonishment, that it was one of the songs that our Heart Sounds International (HSI) team had just finished recording in Erdenet, Mongolia. Apparently, someone had already recorded this new song and a savvy musician computer-notated it just in time to include it in this songbook.

Ken and Dana Davidson and I had just returned from Erdenet, the third largest city of Mongolia, having finished recording with musicians from the Erdenet Jesus Assembly, the nation's largest church. A model for church planting, the assembly had birthed a significant body of worship songs. The previous year, we had recorded eleven of their deeply moving songs. Now in mid-October 2004, we returned to recover tracks of songs that had been damaged in a computer failure.

Quickly humming through the entire songbook, I found a second song from the Erdenet recording in the collection of mostly western and translated songs. The worship leader from Erdenet was ecstatic when I later told him that two of the Erdenet worship songs were on their way across the border into China to strengthen the restricted believers in the underground church of Inner Mongolia.

Reflecting on this, we felt it was not just a pleasant coincidence that the Lord pointed out song number 102. Was there a wider purpose in that special moment? We began to imagine the possibilities of Mongolians releasing songbooks of entire Mongolian-bred songs to enable musicians to teach new indigenous worship songs to congregations.

Before heading back to the capital, Ken had videotaped two of the worship team leaders. He asked them how the worship songs were birthed. One woman said that when she attended the first HSI songwriting event in 2002, she was challenged to write a song. She cried out to the Lord for help, and before long, desperation turned to joy as the new song began to flow.

Another lady told of the unbearable pain and trial she experienced in her home. She had felt a deep need to experience the love of Jesus in a greater way. A Swedish missionary, who had helped plant the church, prayed over her. He prophetically declared that God would release worship songs that expressed his intense love for her. Several of the recorded Erdenet songs demonstrated the powerful melodic and lyrical gifts of this woman of God.

Arriving back in Ulan Bator, the capital, we rejoined the rest of our team and helped launch the third New Song Concert, scheduled for a large Assembly of God church. A songwriting fellowship had formed from the previous year's visit. They had written more than twenty powerful songs. On the night of the concert over nine hundred people crowded into the church for yet another standing-room-only event. The concert featured children of all ages who premiered ten new children's songs. Local people told us this was the first time in Mongolian history that new, children's music was featured in a Christian concert.

The remaining fourteen Christian songs included both traditional and contemporary styles. A traditional dance in praise of the Creator was also performed. As in the previous events, Pastor Dugermaa, a prolific composer and musician, skillfully played and sang the traditional songs, using indigenous instruments.

The following day, the HSI members divided into two recording teams. The daunting task of making professional recordings of the songs from the concert, in the four days that remained, began in earnest. Also a few songs from the 2003 events needed re-recording. Ken set up a studio in a meeting room, having covered the walls with borrowed quilts.

Next door, Paul Neeley, HSI ethnomusicology coordinator, had the joy of working in a studio that HSI had helped establish two years before. Fifteen of the twenty-plus songs had been arranged ahead of time by a talented, local composer-arranger. This vastly simplified the instrumental portion of the recording.

Paul contacted musicians who played traditional instruments and encouraged them to add ethnic flavors to various songs. During a lull in one of the recording sessions, Paul displayed his ethnomusicology prowess. He looked at two guitar players, a traditional music throat-singer,* and a Mongolian Bible nearby, wondering what God might inspire with that special mixture. He then worked with the small group to develop a song that combined a blistering rock guitar duet, ethereal arpeggios, and the text of Psalm 100 sung in the traditional Mongolian way, using two types of throat-singing.

Meanwhile, Noeh Vios, Operation Mobilization Mongolia leader, and I moved throughout the capital, setting up appointments and luncheons with Christian leaders. We presented a two-page vision proposal to start a national movement for distribution of the new worship resources. At one luncheon, Pastor Puje, the pastor-songwriter who had begun the songwriting group a year previous, decided to increase their mandate. They would not only continue to birth new songs; they would also find ways to get worship songs from four recording projects to the far corners of the nation.

On Sunday, we attended a church that had been planted by Bat Ultzi, the first missionary sent out from Mongolia. Bat had spent two years on the Operation Mobilization mission ship *Doulos*. On his return, he started Mongolia's first Christian rock band and began mentoring worship musicians.

A member of the band, long-haired Billy, a delightful and energetic worship leader, played drums for part of the service. A majority of the songs were Mongolian translations of Australian imports. But that Sunday, the congregation experienced something historic—incorporating traditional dances into the worship time. Performing in colorful national outfits, they gracefully praised God with their stylized dance movements.

The next day Billy told us he was longing to use traditional Mongolian instruments again, which had been part of his musical training. Ken asked if the traditional dances at the morning church service rekindled that desire. No, it was not the morning service, but the evening New Songs Concert. When Pastor Dugermaa sang those haunting Mongolian melodies accompanied by national instruments, Billy received an expanded mandate from the Lord to include his culture's musical heritage in the Christian music repertoire of Mongolia. To demonstrate his resolve, Billy went into the studio and recorded a song on a local instrument that he had not touched in six years. Our hearts were deeply touched, perhaps more than at any other time on this visit to Mongolia.

Billy's resolve reflects the heartbeat of HSI—a desire to beat in time with the heart of our Creator God, calling his people, nation by nation, tribe by tribe, language by language, to give their artistic expressions, ancient and modern, contemporary and traditional, back to him as worship.

---

*Throat-singing is a technique that creates more than one pitch at the same time through the manipulation of the lips, throat, and vocal cords.

Chapter 37

Indonesia

The Batak Heresy:
The Struggle to Achieve Meaningful Worship
by Catherine Hodges

Students draped in ceremonial Batak cloth proceeded with poise and dignity toward the altar, in step to a form of music with which they were intimately acquainted—but had never before used in Christian worship. These music and dance forms, traditionally performed in weddings, blessings, funerals, and feasts, were bone- and heart-deep familiar to the worshipers, but the actual composition and choreography were new, created for this 1990 Christmas seminary service by a gifted Batak musician and lecturer.

"Heresy!" muttered a fellow lecturer seated next to me. A generation older than the students and old enough to associate the music and dance with animistic worship practices, he shifted uncomfortably in his seat. The dancers circled the holy family and bowed deeply in homage, accompanied by the voices of traditional Batak drum and flute.

As I watched this service at the Batak seminary in Sumatra, Indonesia, I so much wanted to know what was happening in the minds and hearts of the performers and in those of the Batak students and lecturers seated around me. Heresy was one reply. But as the last of the drumbeats died and we emerged from the sanctuary into the underwater-green dusk, a student turned to me and said, "Hearing our music and seeing our dance just now, I truly feel—for the first time—that Jesus came to earth for me, a Batak."

In Theory

I was, of course, discouraged by the lecturer's response and delighted by that of the student. But both responses are valid, both deserve respect, and together they suggest some of the complexities surrounding the use of indigenous music in worship. "Out with the Western; in with the local!" may have a politically, and even theologically, correct ring to it, but it's an oversimplification that is as wrong-headed and paternalistic as insisting that only Western music has a place in worship around the world. The truth is, we must respect the complexities involved as we foster the use of local music in worshiping the One who deserves profoundly authentic devotion from his creatures.

In Practice

What does such musical devotion look like in practice? Over the last six years in the Indonesian Batak church setting described above, my husband Rob has been piecing together the history of worship music in this almost 150-year-old church, asking old people (both church leaders and lay people)—and young—what they remember and what stories they know from before their own time. He asks people how they feel about church music and worship using, as they do now, German liturgy and Western hymns translated into Batak, or sometimes into Indonesian, the national language. He asks the same questions about *traditional* Batak music and observing people's behavior in situations where traditional music is performed.

Communicating Interest and Respect

Rob is also engaging in traditional music himself. He has learned to play a Batak instrument, the *sarune*—a reed instrument that when practiced indoors sounds like a bagpipe at close range. He utterly terrified his family the first time he tried to coax some silken tones out of the instrument. But he's kept at it and has played in traditional ensembles at festivals and outside-of-the-sanctuary church functions.

Besides earning him a reputation—"the white guy with the big nose who can play our music"—this has endeared him to keepers of traditional music lore; has communicated his interest and respect better than anything he could have said; and has been a deep source of personal enjoyment.

Quarterly Publication

Last year Rob and some Batak friends—including pastors, choir directors, and lay people with an interest in worship music—launched a small quarterly publication by and for Batak church musicians. A devotional and educational tool, it encourages using Batak music in worship. It also covers more general music-in-worship concerns, offers a forum for discussing issues such as the "associative meaning tension," as illustrated in the Christmas program reactions. It also addresses questions from the readership about such things as choral festival criteria, choir rehearsal technique, and so forth.

The subscriber list stands at about 150 and response has ranged from curiosity to elation. One chap wrote and said, more or less, "I've been waiting for this magazine all my life!" We see this publication as groundwork for worship that is authentically Batak, flowing out of repentance and renewal—both of which are desperately needed in the Batak church.

This is Rob's passion, both vocationally and avocationally. Does that mean that only someone trained in ethnomusicology is equipped to wrestle with these issues and fashion some sort of practical response? Not according to what we learned from a survey Rob conducted of Overseas Missionary Fellowship (OMF) church planters across Southeast Asia.

His goal was to document situations and problems that respondents face in using indigenous music in worship and witness. More specifically, he wanted to ascertain whether and how an ethnomusicologist might help them and their national partners as they wrestle with these issues.

The 78 percent return rate, in itself, indicated that the survey had hit on a live issue. We were heartened to find our colleagues—with and without background in Western music, and none with specific training in ethnomusicology—energetically wrestling with ethnomusicological concerns. The respondents, in turn, were glad that somebody had thought to ask. Many enclosed a letter with the four-page survey, expanding on their answers to questions, expressing their own feelings about challenges they are facing, and asking for advice. These people are definitely "doing" ethnomusicology.

After looking over the recommendations Rob made based on the data from the surveys, OMF leadership agreed that there are "hot spots" where outside, trained help could be a great boon in handling music issues with sensitivity and in practical aspects of encouraging the local church to use indigenous music. With this in mind, OMF has recently begun working in cooperation with Prairie Bible Institute to establish a program through which Prairie ethnomusicology students can be placed for short-term work with OMFers serving in Asia.

We hope the summer of 1996 will see at least one Prairie ethnomusicology student placed with church planters in a strategic area in the Philippines. She will work in an area deeply resistant to the good news, as well as to the westernization that marks much of Asia in the twentieth century.

Missionaries in the area have observed that the traditional music is largely "proclamational," and thus well suited to evangelism and teaching. One particular style of song is reserved exclusively for passing along news. Might this be the perfect vehicle for the news most worth passing along? What would be involved in creating a song in this style to tell the news about God's Son, Jesus?

The Prairie student is in for the hands-on experience of her life and the missionaries stand to gain some valuable assistance. But what this is mainly about is—not indigenous music—but the glory of God. Psalm 86:9 says, "All the nations you have made will come and worship before you, O Lord; they will bring glory to your name." God is glorified when He receives the authentic response of our deepest being. Such holy and beautiful worship can never be heresy. Rather, it is a taste of the multicultural heaven we will one day share, knowing that Jesus came to earth at Christmas—for the Batak, and for us all.

This article is adapted from a version printed in *Mission Frontiers,* May–August 1996.

Chapter 38

Central Asia

Light in a Forgotten -stan
by Von Newcomb

The light bulb in our ten-by-fifteen-foot practice room at a national conservatory in north Central Asia had burned out a month earlier, and no one had yet cared enough to replace it.

Sunlight, too, died out dispiritingly early every winter day. The approaching darkness always made me all the more aware of the smell of dust- and mold-saturated curtains and chairs, which hadn't been cleaned in who knows how long. After practice, we left the gray concrete, post-Soviet school and make our way through a maze of other even-more-gloomy-in-the-dark concrete buildings to a bus stop. There we became lost in a sea of other nameless people crammed into buses going to unobserved places. All this was a daily, depressing reminder that, to me, the world had forgotten this "unknown" country whose name ends in "-stan."

But on this particular cheerless December day, as we came to the end of our folk group practice, darkness and anonymity were driven back. A beautiful beam of orange light streamed through the small window. And a profound truth was revealed in a new believer's song.

My family and I lived in this "unknown" country for two years, learning the language and studying folk music. One day, a local musician approached me about helping her and some of her believing friends start a folk instrument worship group. This was an exciting opportunity for all of us, but the first time we met, we were also struck with the magnitude of the task. The first question I asked the group was, "So, what are we going to play?"

"We don't know," they replied, "there isn't any Christian folk music in our culture."

Seemingly not a problem for me, I quickly responded, "That's OK, you guys can write some."

"No we can't. In music school, we weren't composition majors."

"Well, I write music, and I didn't even go to music school! If we start praying and you start trying, God will give you the creativity to voice your praise to him."

Agreed, we began and ended our practices with times of prayer, asking God to give songs and melodies that would beautifully express heartfelt praise. We also started learning other folk songs that would help us jell as a musical group, expand our repertoire, and give us an immediate hearing by other locals.

Weeks of playing and praying passed, when one day, I got an unexpected email from my home office:

> . . . I hope you all are doing well over there. By the way, you submitted a project proposal for a recording studio about a year ago. I have someone who would like to give you the full amount ($20,000)!

I was stunned. At the prodding of my team leader, I had written the proposal for the purchase of some recording equipment and sent it to our organization's project proposal team. But since there was no music to record, I never mentioned it to anyone.

As it turned out, a member of our finance department sent both the proposal and our recent prayer letter about the newly formed folk-instrument worship group to someone interested in helping a project in our area of the world. After reading the two documents, the donor then wrote back and asked if they could help make the studio a reality.

So the home office asked, "Do you want the money?"

What a question! Of course, we wanted the money!

But at the time, there were less than one thousand believers in this people group, and our work with musicians was just beginning to take off. There were not yet any original indigenous worship songs to record. And I didn't want the opportunity of recording on fancy western recording equipment to become the believing musicians' motivation for writing music. Also, I wrote the proposal knowing that I had never actually put together a studio. If they did send the money, how would I even know the best way to use it?

So, God and I came to an agreement. I would say "yes" to the money when and if three things happened. First, I would be assured that there would be new worship songs to record; second, God would provide someone to help me spend the money wisely; and third, he would provide someone to train me in how to use the equipment to its full potential. If any one of those three didn't happen, then the equipment would be nothing more than a very expensive paper weight.

The next day around 10:00 AM, one of our believing musicians knocked on my door for a visit and some *chai* tea—nothing unusual about that. So we got out the tea and cookies and talked a while. And then a very surprising question slipped into the conversation.

"Would you like to hear the new song I just wrote?" she asked.

"What did you just say?" Remember, I was still in language learning and wasn't sure of what I just heard.

"I wrote a new worship song. Will you tell me if you think it is good?"

After lifting my jaw off the floor, Gulnara* played a lovely new song that called her people to praise God for the new life only he can bring. As excited as I was about the new song, I was also in turmoil because of my discussions with God the night before. Was *one* song enough for me to check off the first point in my agreement with God—that there would actually be some new worship songs to record?

After Gulnara left, there was a second knock at the door around 1:00 PM, another musician, and another "Would you like to hear a new song I just wrote?"

Hmm, God, are trying to tell me something?

It was also that same December day at about 4:30 PM when the clouds broke open and a beautiful shaft of orange light streamed into our cold practice room right before sundown. It was like a stage light from heaven shining down on Dilbar* who sheepishly introduced her gift.

"You know, I have been thinking about our discussions and prayers about writing new songs for God. And, well, I decided about a month ago I wanted to write a new song for Jesus— to remember his birth—and I finally finished it last night. Would you all like to hear it?"

She then pulled out her *komuz* (the national instrument of her people) and began to sing:

> There is *sewyewnchew* in the city of Bethlehem!
> Rejoice, my people, Jesus the Savior was born!
> God, who is with us, may you be with us forever, Emmanuel.
> Receive your Creator, who came to abide with you.
>
> My God, filled with power, filled with grace,
> His love, oh, how amazingly infinite it is!
> You can hear his invitation always calling your name.
> He has said, "I am the Way, the Truth, and the Life."
>
> My Lord, I am grateful for your Gift.
> God, who has been with us and will be with us forever, giving eternal life,
> Today, we celebrate your birthday with you!
> And, we glorify and rejoice with you.

When she finished, there was not a dry eye in the room. She had announced the arrival of the Savior in a perfect way, unique to her people and customs. In this Central Asian culture, the word *sewyewnchew* introduces news that is extremely special and valuable, such as a child's birth. In fact, when a person enters a room and announces "Sewyewnchew!" everyone stops what they're doing to hear what amazing news it might be. They are even required to give a gift or some money for the privilege of hearing such a treasured announcement.

> There is sewyewnchew in the city of Bethlehem!
> Rejoice, my people, Jesus the Savior was born!

As we sat rejoicing together in the dusty practice room, the golden orange light eventually faded to black. Lost for words, I was overwhelmed with the care and concern of our living, heavenly Father. As Dilbar was singing, it struck me again that these people were on Jesus' heart way back when he came to be the sewyewnchew for the world.

The three new songs arriving miraculously in one day were a clear and direct answer to both our group's prayers and my question—about whether or not a studio would be used in this place. I was sure then that God would bring individuals to help fulfill the second and third parts of our agreement.

Four days later, I met a man who introduced me to a friend who installs studios professionally and who also teaches recording technology at the university level. One year later the studio was up and running.

I still don't like the way darkness falls early in winter in Central Asia. But now, every time I see a sunset in December, I remember that in spite of the disrepair and hopelessness all around me, this "-stan" has never been forgotten by the only One who can bring to it light and hope.

Epilogue

The song "Sewyewnchew" was recorded in spring 2000, along with the other firstfruits of worship from these musicians, and was released in a collection called *Kudaidy Danktaibuz* ("We Glorify God"). A second recording of original spiritual songs and melodies entitled *Baysal* (the chosen name of the folk ensemble) was completed using the new recording equipment in 2003.

In 2005, at the time this article was written, the Baysal musicians were still playing together. A group of them are currently recording a collection of original modern instrument worship songs they, and other musicians in their church's worship team, have written. This recording is being co-produced by the author of this article and the leader of Baysal who is learning how to run the studio.

*The name has been changed to protect the person's identity.

Chapter 39

Colorado, USA

Ute Grandma Sings for God and Her People
by Nola Shoemaker

Anna's grandma often left the house in the evening and climbed the hill to look over the river to the bluff beyond. She would watch the sun set, sing, and sometimes chant a prayer, as she sought—in her own way—the Creator's help.

Anna Bettini, now an 84-year-old grandmother herself, has retained those tunes that floated over the valley to the opposite cliffs, even though the words are now indistinct. A Ute woman and a glowing Christian, Anna has become an ardent composer of Christian music in the Ute language.

Born on a sagebrush flat along the Animas River, south of Durango, Colorado, Anna was raised during the depression on a farm, which included sheep and horses. Her house and its nearby horse corrals were fashioned of native materials. She traveled by horse and wagon.

Anna, her sister, father, and "grandmother"—in truth, a great aunt—survived on what they could find: cedar berries, native plants, rabbits, and their sheep. Accompanying their grandma up into the hills to let the sheep graze, the girls cared for lambs, picked berries, made their own toys from clay, wood, or ears of corn, and made up their own games.

Because of their isolation, the family did not attend Ute ceremonies: bear dances, sun dances, and pow-wows. Ute religious beliefs tied them closely to nature, including many animals and birds, such as the eagle, buffalo, wolf, and bear.

Anna attended boarding school with other Native American children, and later joined the armed services, serving her country stateside. She married, but later after her husband died, she went back to school, earned her teaching degree, and taught for many years, including teaching Ute reading and writing to children in all twelve grades. A respected and loved elder among her people, Anna was named Colorado's "Woman of the Year" in 1988.

She also worked in linguistics, helping Dr. Tom Givon write the first Ute dictionary, grammar, and book of Ute folk stories, recorded by Ute elders (published in 1976).

In the fall of 1987, Anna joined the Ute Translation Committee, working with me and my husband, Jack, and others. Along with Bible translation, she translated hymns and choruses into Ute and sang them.

In 2001 when she was eighty years old, Anna attended ethnomusicology workshops where she, along with other Native American people, began composing and recording songs to their own tunes. She also recited her testimony and Scriptures to background music, sometimes a low-pitched, beautiful chant sung by another Ute lady, Betty Howe.*

The tunes and rhythms Anna had heard from her grandmother at sunset long ago returned to her and provided rich, authentic material for her creations. "From Emptiness to Glory" is a beautiful, soul-stirring chant to one of those tunes.

> Before I knew the Lord, I was empty;
> I was searching for a better life;
>
> . . .
>
> Now I am redeemed; I have Salvation.
> I have hope that I may one day enter into his glory.
> I will no longer be empty—I will be full of his glory.

I will one day live in that glorious place with him,
Where I have come from emptiness to glory!

The Lord often gave Anna a tune, to which she would add words of her testimony, or a spontaneous praise to the Lord, or a psalm. One of the first songs she recorded was based on Psalm 15: "LORD, who may dwell in your sanctuary? Who may live on your holy hill?" The chorus in Ute script looks like this:

> Heyanaa, Heyanaa, Heya Heyoo;
> Núumarogumapügat, iní urú?u
> Ümüí kaní-naagai káaka-paatüm?
> Iní urú?u Ümüí kaní-naagatug unípüwi-paatüm?
> Heyanaa, Heyanaa, Heya Heyo

Another song was composed from an Eskimo lady's testimony in which she praises God that she is a child of the King. It is considered an "honor song" to that lady.

> Heyajaa Heyajaa Heyajaa
> We are the children of the King;
> We are the children of the Living God.
> Do not be discouraged,
> Do not be dismayed, neither be afraid!
> Saith the Lord God of Israel.
> Jajajáaa jajajáaa jajajáaa jajájajá

Recently, in the middle of the night, Anna wanted to sleep but was not able to because praise lyrics kept going through her mind, even as her feet danced under the covers. She knew she should get up and record the song, but she was weary.

But Lord, I am tired; I want to sleep! she objected.

"You need to record it now; by morning it will fade away," the Lord replied in her heart. So at 2:30 AM, Anna got up, tape-recorded her song, and the next day, wrote it down.

Anna keeps a well-ordered notebook full of handwritten poems she is composing or revising. When she is finally satisfied with one, her daughter or I enter it into a computer. When a tune for those lyrics comes to Anna, she records and memorizes it. Later she has it professionally recorded and added to her CD, two hundred of which she has already sold or given away.

Anna's heart is so full of praise to the Lord that the songs just spill out. She is able to create and sing a children's or literacy song—on the spot—translating into Ute a short text that someone suggests, and finding a tune that fits the lyrics well. Anna has had this gift for many years and has used it in her teaching career.

For several years, Anna was disturbed by derogatory comments about Indian music and chanting. She often said, "I'm so tired of hearing people say our Indian music is inferior, or of the devil." Anna knows what types of Ute music are appropriate for hymns of praise. Speed and combinations of chant syllables make the difference—a system only the Ute people fully understand. In addition, ethnomusicologists knowledgeable about many different styles of music have helped Anna use her God-given talent—freely—to praise the Lord.

In 2004, Anna translated Psalm 92 into Ute:

Psalm 92:14–15

Even in old age I will do good;
I will not become weary;
I will be strong; I will say:
God is good,
He is strong and stable like a big rock.
Everything that he does is good;
He cannot think evil;
He shepherds me.

Nüʔ wíitapü-vaisüp túüʔunívaat
Nüʔ urá kach wüwúnüvaauwat;
Súügaivaat. Nüʔ máivaat:
"Máa Núumarogumapügatü túüʔaitüm,

Avátü tüpüíchi úpanan wünútikyat.
Paámanöni uwáias urá?n túü?ait.
Uwás ka-üvúü sumái?niwat,
Tamó?inigean. "

Anna knows her Creator is pleased with her song and chant offerings, rising to heaven in praise. As the psalm says, even in old age, the Lord shepherds this former shepherdess and strengthens her to do good— singing for God and her people.

*Betty Howe has translated many hymns into Ute and sings them at church services and funerals. She has made CDs of Ute singing and has drawn other people into singing and reciting Ute Scriptures to background music. An outspoken Christian, she won a seat on the tribal council, which has helped her introduce more people to Christian literature, CDs, and videos in Ute.

Chapter 40

Philippines

"Semi-Tribal" Songs Unite Generations
by Glenn Stallsmith

"Why would you want us to use our language? We don't even like it ourselves!"

When Robert and Margaret Hunt arrived in Mindanao, Philippines, in 1989, they told the Matigsalug Manobo community they wanted to translate the Scriptures into their language. The people were incredulous.

Many Matigsalugs questioned the Hunts' motives. Caught between their own traditional way of life and those of the dominating Cebuano lowlanders, the Matigsalugs had trouble defining exactly who they were as a people. This was an especially difficult problem for the Matigsalug believers. The only Christians they knew were outsiders—lowlander Cebuanos. In fact, the word *Kristiano* is synonymous with "lowlanders." In order to be a Christian, the Matigsalugs thought, one must become like the lowlanders, adopting their language, culture, and even their styles of clothing.

Despite the opposition, Robert and Margaret persevered. Over the years, they taught from the Bible how God wanted the Matigsalugs to honor him with their culture and language. In time, the Matigsalug Christians began to value their own cultural forms and embrace their traditional ways that were compatible with scriptural truth. In the process they established local organizations that were directed by Matigsalugs:

the Matigsalug Christian Language Association and the Matigsalug Literacy Education Incorporated.

In early 2005, I had the opportunity to meet with some Matigsalug Christians who wanted to create new songs for worshiping God. Because of the Hunts' and other translators' commitment and work, the churches already had two books of worship songs with Matigsalug language texts. But most of these songs sung in the churches used tunes from other culture groups—English language hymns, Filipino choruses, and others.

We spent one week together in a workshop, exploring ways to create totally new songs comprised of Matigsalug words and new melodies. The participants were eager to write their own songs and began doing so on the first day.

Two young men who came were gifted in composing songs that uniquely blended traditional and modern elements. They called their style "semi-tribal." On the first day, they shared a song that used a *modern* seven-note scale for the verse and a *traditional* chant in the chorus. These two new believers were serious students of their culture. They even led some of the young people in traditional dances. Their "semi-tribal" songs had a special way of uniting Matigsalugs of all generations. There were enough modern elements to appease the young while retaining traditional components that satisfied the older generation.

The workshop concluded on Friday afternoon with a concert of songs composed during the week. As the participants gathered, dressed in traditional Matigsalug outfits, Robert Hunt said, "This never would have happened fifteen years ago. The Christians were too ashamed to wear their traditional clothing."

One of the pastors who had participated in the workshop opened the concert with an *uranda*, an extemporaneous traditional song used to greet visitors and relate news.

At the end of the week, thirteen songs had been recorded and were ready for distribution throughout the language area. Since the time of the workshop, media specialists have helped the Hunts produce and distribute cassette tapes from these recordings. A Christian family in the main Matigsalug settlement has installed an outside speaker and now plays Matigsalug Christian music to the entire neighborhood.

A recent Christian Talent Night held during the Matigsalug fiesta, a wholesome alternative to the secular activities, featured a new category this year: original compositions. Several churches entered this category, and so the new songs continue. The Hunts plan to build an audio recording studio in the language area in late 2005 to produce radio programs and cassette tapes with Matigsalug songs.

As we have seen happen elsewhere in the Philippines, the Matigsalug song-writing workshop brought energy into this dynamic translation project. It helped identify talented people previously unknown to the translators. It also highlighted the translation and literacy work for some Matigsalugs who were previously unaware of these activities. We praise God that he continues to raise up unique Matigsalug forms of worship for his glory.

Chapter 41

Papua New Guinea

Authentic Alamblak Worship

by Neil Coulter

"You must get rid of everything associated with your traditional religious practices. If you don't, these things will destroy your entire language group." This is what Alamblak speakers of Papua New Guinea's East Sepik province understood early missionaries were telling them.

Because of a language barrier between the Alamblak people and expatriate missionaries, what could have been an opportunity for discussion and discernment turned into a seemingly dogmatic ultimatum. During the 1960s and 1970s, many Alamblak people turned away from traditional religious practices, burning artifacts associated with those beliefs and embraced the Christian church. Within the walls of local churches, worship included European and American hymns in English or Tok Pisin, Papua New Guinea's lingua franca (trade language), but seldom heard was the Alamblak language, and never, local musical styles. Christians accepted the new practices of the church and put away their traditional music. This continued throughout the early years of the church.

Then in 2003, many Alamblak people attended a church course on music in the Bible. They were surprised to find that the Bible has much to say about music—and not just about church music, but music covering all aspects of daily life.

On the second day of the course, facilitators encouraged participants to think about their own culture's music. They brainstormed, pinpointing all their local music styles, and wrote them on a chalkboard. Then they considered among themselves what styles might be suitable for use in Christian worship. After discussion, people concluded that *refonm*—a style featuring vocals accompanied by the *kundu*, an hourglass-shaped, single-membrane drum—would do well for praising God.

Some people interested in new Christian songs felt unsure about how to compose them. However, in the week following the course, several Alamblak people composed new Christian refonm songs. One of these new songs came to the composer in a dream, which further affirmed that Christian songs in refonm style were good. The new song lyrics recounted God's love for humanity, the work of Jesus coming to earth and dying for sins, and various Bible stories, including David fighting Goliath.

The excitement and enthusiasm people exhibit as they perform these new, culturally-appropriate Christian songs—during all-night worship events—is almost tangible. No outsiders composed any of the songs, wrote any of the lyrics, or suggested any of the Bible verses or themes used in the songs. This is truly authentic Alamblak Christian worship.

Today many Alamblak Christians are finding a freedom they have not known before. As they continue to compose new Christian songs, they understand that God cares about their unique music, and that he enjoys praise in any spoken or musical language.

"We feel ashamed at how much of our local music has already been lost," says Alamblak councilman Fransis Jeri, "but now we know that God is pleased with our own music. Now we can discern what from our past was good and what was evil. We must preserve what is good and turn it into praise to God."

Encore:
Reflection
and Response

Chapter 42

Bolivia

Music Ministry, Take Two:
What I'd Do Differently
by Rolly Walter

Israel showed up at Hebrón Seminary in search of music lessons. He was a Guaraní from southeastern Bolivia, and his church had sent him to Santa Cruz to learn all he could from the new seminary music teacher.

Israel wanted to play the keyboard so, like every good music teacher should, I started him with simple songs, learning to read by notes. Then I moved him to scales—still from a book. At first he was eager to learn and gave it a good try. Soon, though, he started to lose interest. Before the month was up, he had gone back home. Israel had lots of musical talent, but to him music was sounds and hand positions. It had nothing to do with markings on a page. His church wanted him to accompany songs on a keyboard, and I tried to teach him music theory and sight-reading.

Adhemar was also a talented musician. He was a seminary student who served as the music leader in a large church. When he registered for my advanced theory class, I was excited because I knew he would excel. I tried to teach him how to harmonize a melody and how to write an accompaniment part. It took me a while to realize that he didn't really see the point of it all. No one else in his church would be able to read the music he wrote. He played and sang by ear, and so did everyone else.

When I went to Santa Cruz, Bolivia, to teach music at Hebrón Theological Seminary, I felt I was qualified to jump right in and begin teaching. I have a degree in music, and I had gained practical experience in a church. I was raised in South America and already knew how to speak the language. I was familiar with many of the Spanish hymns and choruses, and I knew what Latin American church music was all about. I was eager to have an impact on church music in Bolivia.

It didn't take long for me to become aware of my misconceptions. I was ready to introduce contemporary praise and worship music to Bolivian churches, but that's about all most churches were singing. I wanted to introduce worship teams, but the church we began attending already had one. I was prepared to teach all the musical skills necessary for good church music but found that much of what I brought with me from North America wasn't practical.

As a seminary teacher, I had a captive audience, so my students had to learn what I taught them if they wanted to pass the required music class. I drilled them on half notes and quarter notes. They learned the names of lines and spaces on a staff. They learned what a time signature is. They learned scales. Everyone in class had to direct a song using the correct hand motions. In choir everyone had to read from printed sheet music. They had to research the circumstances behind the writing of numerous hymns.

However, I don't think I saw much of what I taught about music theory put into practice in church. The students took from my classes only what was useful to their ministries. My guitar students helped lead singing for Awana and youth meetings. Some of my choir members discovered their voices and started singing in church. One student started a children's choir and taught songs she had learned from me. Others used the chorus book with guitar chords I had compiled to accompany singing or to teach someone else to play. Worship leaders started putting more thought into the content and flow of the music they selected. I did have an impact, but not in the way I had expected.

So what would I do differently? Instead of trying to teach what I had learned in my university courses, I would try to be more practical, even if it meant giving up some of my musical ideals. For instance, four-part music would be out because Latin American music mainly uses three parts, and few men care to sing bass. The chorus book I compiled should have included diagrams of finger positions for keyboards, but I didn't include them because it was beneath me. My background taught me people should learn to play the piano with sheet music, but how useful is that when there is very little printed music available? Playing by ear is a much more useful skill. I'm not a big fan of programmed rhythms and accompaniments on keyboards, but that's what Israel's church wanted. I would teach him to use them well.

Maybe Israel and Adhemar learned something practical from me, and maybe someday they will benefit from my music theory lessons. But I would have had a much greater contribution to the music in their churches if my classes had focused less on what I thought a "good" musician should know and more on what would serve their churches.

This article originally appeared in *The Gospel Message,* 1999:3, pp. 4–5.

Chapter 43

Togo

Catalytic Composers Spark God's Praise

by Paul Neeley

At a month-long workshop for creating psalms, the most prolific and zealous participants weren't even supposed to be there. They were strangers, replacements, invited at the last minute.

In 1996, language groups in Togo and Benin had been invited to send representatives to the workshop, preferably a translator and composer from each group.

The Ifè translation team was not able to attend the whole workshop because translating Psalms was not then a priority in their project goals. Nevertheless, they hoped that if an Ifè composer took part in the workshop, some indigenous church music might be encouraged. They saw this as a real need for better communication of the gospel, since Ifè churches usually borrowed songs from larger ethnic groups.

A composer was invited, but had to back out at the last minute. Someone suggested Koku, who was willing to come. He even brought a friend, Meesa.

Koku, Meesa, and I rode six hours together to the northern Togo workshop center. Pat Devine, a member of the Ifè team, translated my questions into Ifè even as she dodged potholes. I got a "feel for the land,"

and we shared some ideas. We talked, ate, and dozed, wondering just what God intended to do during the week ahead.

The following morning, Koku and Meesa arose early, eager to get started. They had already made a song from Psalm 5:1–3 (a passage I had mentioned in the car the day before). Tapping a syncopated rhythmic pattern on a Coke bottle (one usually played on an iron bell), they sang in a call-and-response form with typical Ifè harmony (a fourth below the melody). They were so enthused with their effort and liked the words so much that they made two arrangements of the same lyrics in two musical genres.

During the workshop we discussed all of the genres of Ifè music, exploring the potential fit of certain ones with biblical lyrics. We saw there were a number of appropriate options available within the heart music system of the Ifè culture.

You've never seen ducks taking to water the way these two young guys took to indigenous hymnody. We discussed making songs for a cassette recording of the Christmas story. The next day I heard the first Ifè Christmas song:

> A promise was made to Mary;
> She was told she would give birth to a son.
> He will save the world and be called Jesus.

Then we roughed out a script for a cassette recording of Genesis 1–3. The next day they sang a creation song:

> God, God created man.
> When God finished making the world,
> He said, "Let's make man in our image."
> God took some earth
> And he fashioned it in the shape of man,
> And when he had finished shaping it,
> He breathed into its nose, and it became man.
> God, God created man.

They tried their hand at gospel scenes:

Jesus says, "Come down, Zaccheus, come down!
Come down from the tree, and let's go home.
The Lord has come to you today.

They turned their attention to verses from the epistles:

Humble yourselves, humble yourselves before God.
God will lift you up.

They made songs from their experience growing up in the traditional religion:

They don't give life.
The eaters of goats and sheep sacrifices—
They don't ever give life.
The gods have eyes, but their eyes don't see.
The gods have ears, but their ears don't hear.

They took the vow expressed by Ruth to Naomi and made it into a beautiful *gudugba* song:

Where you go, I will also go;
Where you live, it is there that I also will live;
Your people will be my people;
Your God will be my God.

In a week's time at the workshop, Koku and Meesa had made fourteen new songs. Two months later, a set of five cassettes in the Ifè language was recorded. Two tapes were filled with twenty-two songs composed by the gifted duo. They were lively, accompanied with drums, bells, rattles, and calabashes (how could anyone not dance?). Three other cassettes contained dramatizations, preaching, and testimonies, interspersed with more songs.

They put together a performing ensemble and went from church to church to introduce the songs and have discussions about indigenous hymnody. They caught the vision of what an impact such hymnody could have both within the church service and in evangelization of the Ifè people. The flame was lit and burned brightly. The last day of the workshop, Koku said, "We came blind, but now we see." He asked us to pray that God would really do things through these songs among his people.

Composers from the other six language groups also responded well to the challenge put forth at the workshop. A total of fifty new songs were composed that week. But the Ifè composers—the replacements—excelled and surpassed them all.

I'm glad God is in control.

As the new Ifè song says,

> You are God, you have great power;
> You have raised the dead.
> You have opened the ears of the deaf
> And the eyes of the blind.
> You have spoken to the waters and they obeyed;
> You have spoken to the evil spirits and they were humbled.
> You are God.
> You are God.

Soon after the first set of cassettes was released, some Ifè people on their way home from working in the fields were attracted by the sound of music nearby. They left the path to see what was going on. One of the new cassettes of Ifè music was playing, so they all sat down to listen.

Next they heard a tape of Christian testimonies in the Ifè language. As a result of these tapes, several of them became Christians! The owner of the cassettes was not even a Christian himself; he had bought them because they used his language and music.

Later, five more Ifè cassettes were recorded, and people have come to know Christ by the hundreds through this ministry, including leaders in the traditional religion. Pray for further fruit among the Ifè people of Togo as the gospel is communicated in forms they understand and appreciate.

You are God, you have great power.
You are God.
You are God.

This article was first published in *EM News* 5:3, 1996. That issue also contains a more formal ethnomusicological article, "A Summary of Ifè Music in Relation to Church Use" in which Pat Devine and Ifè colleagues describe briefly the almost thirty genres of Ifè music and examine them for potential suitability within a Christian context.

March 2006 update: Kokou is now an Assembly of God pastor and still composes music. The latest cassette he recorded was a set of sixteen songs taken from verses in Hebrews. The entire book of Hebrews was recently recorded with songs interspersed at appropriate points in the text.

Chapter 44

Togo

Music, Drama, and Storying*:
Exciting Foundations for Church Planting
by Tom Ferguson

By the year 2000, the fruit of hymnody workshops held in Togo in 1996 and 1997 had multiplied. Ifè speakers continued composing Christian music using indigenous musical styles. Several believers discovered a gift for composing, and some churches had begun organizing music groups.

Ifè Baptist leadership desired to learn how to more effectively use their music in evangelism and approached me, an IMB** "indigenous music catalyst," for help.

At the same time, local believers discussed with IMB workers Jess and Peggy Thompson the need for ways to reach adults with the gospel. The Thompsons wanted them to see that any Christian can be a church planter.

In March 2000, a four-day workshop on music evangelism and church planting was held for sixty Ifè believers in Morétan, Togo. The focus was two-fold: the importance of using indigenous methods for evangelism and recognizing that God had already equipped churches for the task. God had been preparing His people for this event, and we were eager to see what He was going to do.

Each session began with praise, using Ifè indigenous Christian music, and prayer for villages that had no gospel witness. Then a local pastor or evangelist emphasized the importance of every believer sharing his or her faith and helping start new churches.

An elderly Ifè woman set the example. Several times she had been sent away by her husband because of her vibrant faith in Jesus. She remained faithful to the Lord, however, and continued sharing her beliefs in various villages. Since she had no one to teach her, she bought a Bible ("with my own money") and had someone read to her. She told workshop participants, "I know nothing of paper (she is not literate). I just told people the Bible lessons that others had taught me."

She also created songs about biblical truths and taught them to all who would listen. Gathering village children around her daily, she taught them about God. As a result of her faithfulness, three Ifè churches were started.

The workshop taught culturally-appropriate evangelism techniques and also provided opportunities to apply them. Participants were organized into four working groups. Each group was to create a presentation of a Bible story using storytelling, drama, indigenous music styles, and dance. On Wednesday morning each group made its presentation to the others, who expressed their appreciation and offered suggestions for improvement. The afternoon was reserved for perfecting their work for a later presentation in a village.

On Wednesday evening we gathered for a time of prayer and spiritual preparation before taking the message to the people of Fodjaye and Tchekele villages.

On Thursday morning we celebrated what God had done in the villages and throughout the workshop. The Ifè believers were excited about how they were received. Young and old came out to hear what they had to present and invited them to return. They were eager to get home and begin using this method of sharing God's Word with others.

In their own words, here are the principles the Ifè learned about cross-cultural evangelism through music, song, and drama:

Recognize and Honor the Authorities of the Village

"In Tchekele, we sent a delegation to see the chief. We discovered that there had been a death in his family, and we gave our condolences."

"In Fodjaye, the chief heard us dancing and was pleased, so he sent us drinks to encourage us."

Get the Villagers' Attention First

"Find out what type of dance a village likes before going, and then use it."

"People came out when they heard the drums. This is a good method to gather people."

"People preparing food left it on the fire and came out without eating!"

"People danced more than we did. When we stopped, they said it was not enough."

"People were pleased. There was so much dancing that they brought water to put on the ground to keep the dust down."

"Before this, many people had doubts [about using certain local customs for worship purposes]. People wondered, *If I become a Christian, can I still dance* àgbàdzà*?* We have shown them that you can dance and still be Christian."

Avoid Looking and Sounding like a Church

"We didn't do anything 'churchy' like saying 'Hallelujah!' or praying. We just started making music. At first the people didn't realize that we were Christians, and then they recognized some of us. They were surprised when they saw who was doing this."

"We told the story without the Bible in hand; this was effective. Many times when people see the Bible brought out, they leave. It is good to memorize God's Word so you don't have to hold a Bible."

Drama Holds People's Attention

"When we stopped dancing, some people wanted to leave because they thought we were going to start preaching. When they found out we were going to do a drama, they stayed!"

"We told them we had a drama to present first before dancing some more. We presented 'Cain and Abel,' then danced. Even the old came out to dance. The other group then presented 'Abraham sacrifices Isaac.'"

"Drama is a good way to explain the Word. Compared to the 'old way' of evangelism, this is better. People used to leave when the prayer and preaching started. Now they want us to return."

"People were touched by the drama. They understood the message."

Songs Present the Message in a Non-Threatening Way

"Some of the songs touched the people deeply. They were surprised and convicted."

"The songs preached the Word and touched the people."

"This is a good method. It is effective. People listen to songs when they won't listen to preaching."

Using Local Instruments Gives a Positive Message

"People thought we were there with the Bible. When we asked for àgbàdzà drums, they were surprised. A villager played the gourd shaker."

Some People in a Village Will Lend Their Support

"Some people were waiting. They knew we were coming. We didn't have drums. Seven drums were brought out by the villagers for us to use."

"People were waiting when we arrived. Many participated in the dance. People were proud and happy. A young man from the village helped us with the drumming."

"The few Christians in the village were encouraged to see that they could also do this."

"Christians from the (second) village were encouraged to use this method."

Discover What Works within the Culture

"Going out as a group was good too. People were astonished. Before, just the missionary or evangelist came to share with them. People came out to see the *yovo* (white person), thinking they could profit in some way by their presence."

"We have learned how to use our own methods and resources. God is not foreign to us. He understands us."

"It is not that we don't praise God in our churches, but we have done it with foreign methods. Now we can use our own."

"The old way of evangelism through preaching does not attract people. This method is good. We need to ask, 'How can I do this in my village or church?' because people are interested. We didn't pray or preach, yet the people were interested."

Plans for the Future

"Form a group to perform every Sunday so the church can get accustomed to this. Instead of using a brass band, we need to show we have our own methods. We need an àgbàdzà group to serve as a model."

"As for imported or foreign songs, others taught us or composed them for us. We need to find our own local composers. We recognize that not everyone has the gift to compose."

"Everything is learned. We need to try to put these things into practice to find out. If we sit with our arms crossed we will do nothing. If we don't try, we will not discover our gifts."

The grandma mentioned earlier sang her advice: "My *pagne* (wraparound skirt) is what we Ifè women like to wear, my necklace also is Ifè. We need to use what comes from our Ifè people."

To implement these plans, the participants organized several one-day seminars throughout the region. They wanted to demonstrate the principles they had learned to all the churches in their association. The Bible story music-dramas were perfected and presented outside, under a tree, near the church building. One seminar happened to take place during market day. When villagers heard the music begin, the market place emptied as they came to enjoy it. The participants saw first-hand the power of culturally-appropriate music to draw a crowd.

Many church delegations returned home and created indigenous music-drama groups. Within four months after the Ifè churches were introduced to culturally-appropriate evangelism using oral methods, ten new Bible studies and worship gatherings were established. In two of the villages, the chiefs had previously not permitted any Christian witness or activity at all.

One church music group reported that when they used music, drama, and storying to present the gospel, villagers always asked them to return. That church group leader wrote a note to the association's evangelist stating, "Using music and drama allows everyone to participate in evangelism." It is remarkable how new Scripture songs can gain a hearing for the gospel and play a major part in a church-planting effort.

Many Ifè Christians are learning that it's not "put down the written Bible and pick up the drum," but "put the Bible in your memory and heart with the aid of songs, then pick up the drum and share with your neighbors."

*Storying is telling Bible stories in an intentional order for the purpose of evangelization, church planting, and so forth.

**International Mission Board of the Southern Baptist Convention

---

Originally published in *EM News,* 9:1, 2000.

Chapter 45

Asia

Artists Hold Keys
to Unreached People Groups
by John Oswald

Where are the tellers of parables, proverbs, and well-crafted stories?

Where are the singers of songs, ballads, and epics?

Where are the visual artists who, by a few strokes of a pen or brush, can sum up a thousand words?

Dedicated Christian artists have far more to offer than they realize when it comes to breaking through barriers that block communication of the gospel. In many cultures, three-point sermons often don't fit! Artists have the keys to thousands of unreached ethnic groups, each with an amazing and distinct culture.

Some years ago, I participated in a local amateur song and dance group in a small Asian city. Learning to play their most distinctive folk instrument, a long-necked lute with six strings, I rehearsed with them, drank tea with them, sat in on their group discussions, and eventually participated in performances with them.

My interest in their lute gave me entry to this circle. Among other things, I discovered that music—for them—is only *one* facet of their performing arts. They do not see a dichotomy between music and dance, drama and song. Each part contributes to the whole, and what results is a highly colorful, energetic, and exhilarating all-round performance.

I also learned what my musical interest in their culture meant to them. A complete stranger's comment summed it up: "You have come from a foreign land and have learned our language and culture. That touches my heart."

My personal involvement in their music equipped me to fill a hole in this small Christian community's worship life—but the scope is unlimited. Christian artists prepared to learn the arts of such unreached peoples will discover new horizons for communication. This work calls for people with varied skills, including music, dance, and the dramatic arts. It does not require a research degree, though this might be helpful.

It especially takes a willingness to learn a new way of thinking, culturally and artistically, and most of all, a desire to communicate the love of Christ to a fallen world. If we lay aside our cultural pride and, like our Savior, associate with people in the ways that are meaningful to them, it will touch their hearts—not just for a performance, but also for their eternal destiny.

This article was adapted from one written for the British journal, *Worship Together*. It was later published in *EM News* 7:4, 1998.

Author Biographies

Phil Anderson

Phil Anderson is an Avant missionary in Bamako, the capital city of Mali, West Africa. He and his wife, Ev, have served thirty-nine years in French ministry and in the Avant Ministries (formerly Gospel Missionary Union) Literature Production Center.

Ron Binder

Ron and Kathy Binder, with Wycliffe Bible Translators, have worked with the Wounaan since 1970. Besides completing the New Testament, they have published over fifty books in the language. They are currently assigned to Wycliffe mobilization in California, but have recently responded to an invitation from Wounaan church leaders to help produce outreach materials. The Binders now work with two Wounaan men, facilitating projects via email, and travel to Panama twice a year. The development of culturally-appropriate hymns continues to be a priority for the Wounaan.

Carol Brinneman

Carol Brinneman joined Wycliffe Bible Translators in 1970 and worked in Bible translation and literacy in Côte d'Ivoire, and later Togo. She assisted her husband, Neal, and team in completing the translation of the New Testament for the Lama people of northern Togo; it was dedicated in 1994. Since then, they have worked at JAARS, the technical hub for Wycliffe in Waxhaw, North Carolina. Carol is presently editor of the JAARS magazine: *Rev. 7 Every Nation People Language.* Carol is also a freelance writer; many articles on her life experiences are posted at: www.wysite.org/sites/brinnemans.

Karen Campbell

Karen Campbell, originally from Northern Ireland, taught music at Daystar University in Nairobi, Kenya, from 1998–2001. There she came into contact with refugees from Sudan and began to study their music for her master's thesis. Karen is presently a minister with the Presbyterian Church in Ireland. She recently completed another master's thesis on a theology of music from a reformed perspective. Her husband, David, is a teacher and also a keen musician.

Neil Coulter

Neil and Joyce Coulter work as ethnomusicologists with SIL in Papua New Guinea.

Ken Davidson

Ken Davidson has served as a director of worship for many years, involving numerous church plants, as well as leading conferences and seminars. Combined graduate studies in theology and music led him to blend pastoral ministries and worship leadership. Ken is a co-founder of Heart Sounds International (HSI). He joined Operation Mobilization in order to focus more on HSI needs. He has participated in mission projects in the Philippines, Mongolia, Guatemala, Brazil, the Dominican Republic, South Africa, Senegal, Tunisia, India, the Maldives, and Sri Lanka. Ken has completed three CD recordings of his own compositions, but his greatest passion is to help develop worship in the church around the world. Ken is based in the Kansas City area where he resides with his wife, Dana. They have three grown sons.

Paul H. DeNeui

Paul H. DeNeui holds a PhD in Intercultural Studies. He has spent eighteen years enabling indigenous organizations to facilitate holistic and culturally relevant ministries that direct people to Christ within the context of a folk Buddhist country in Southeast Asia. At present, he is the associate professor of Mission and director of the Center for World Christian Studies at North Park Theological Seminary, Chicago.

Leticia Dzokotoe

Leticia and Dan Dzokotoe worked as non-print media specialists and recording engineers with the Ghana Institute of Linguistics, Literacy, and Bible Translation, an affiliate of SIL. Leticia died in 2005 and is sorely missed by many.

Tom Ferguson

Tom Ferguson has served as an indigenous music catalyst with the International Mission Board of the Southern Baptist Convention since December 1994. After language school in France, he and his wife, Tina, worked in West Africa for 9 ½ years. While there, Tom conducted Scripture-based song workshops for thirty people groups in six countries. Tina assisted in recording and producing the more than seventy cassette tapes and CDs that resulted from the workshops.

The Fergusons currently serve in South Asia. Tom is an indigenous music catalyst and leader of the Creative Arts Strategy Team. One of his roles is music facilitator/mentor for the OneStory Partnership teams working in Asia. Tina serves as audio/video project manager for the South Asia media team. Tom holds music degrees from the University of Southern Mississippi and Southwestern Baptist Theological Seminary. He is a charter member of the International Council of Ethnodoxologists.

Frank Fortunato

Frank Fortunato taught college music for several years before joining Operation Mobilization (OM) in 1972. He served many years on board the OM mission ships, *Logos* and *Doulos*. Currently, Frank is OM's international music director, coordinating Heart Sounds International, a ministry that encourages and enables indigenous worship recordings in restricted parts of the world. Based at the OM USA headquarters in Atlanta, Frank also leads worship at area churches, conducts music and worship seminars, and is an adjunct teacher on world music at a Christian college. Frank's wife, Berit, from Sweden, teaches elementary grades. They have two grown children and two adopted children from India.

Sue Hall

Sue Hall, PhD, serves with Pioneers as a church planter and ethnomusicologist among the Wolof people of West Africa. The music of Africa has fascinated her since she served as an intern with Wycliffe Bible Translators in Ghana in 1996 and saw the power of Scripture set to local music to transform the life and worship of African believers. You can email Sue at suerachel@emailglobe.net.

Dave and Kay Henry

Dave and Kay Henry have served with InterAct Ministries in Yakutsk, northern Siberia since 1993. They assist the emerging Yakut church in developing Christian literature, such as the Yakut hymnal, *Tangaragha Aikhal* ("Praise to God"), with 120 translated and original songs, including one Christian ohuokai, published in 2002. They formerly served as Bible translators with Wycliffe with the Koyukon Athabaskan people of Alaska.

Pat Ham

Pat Ham joined Wycliffe Bible Translators in 1957 and worked with the Apinayé from 1959–1970 and 1986–2000. She is now retired and doing volunteer work at Wycliffe's southeast regional office in Stone Mountain, Georgia.

Robin Harris

Robin Harris and her husband, Bill, have served with InterAct Ministries in Russia since 1994. While living in Siberia, Robin became fascinated with Sakha music and began to study ethnomusicology. She earned an MA in Intercultural Studies from Columbia International University and an MA in ethnomusicology from Bethel University in 2006. In 2003, she founded the International Council of Ethnodoxologists (ICE) with a team of like-minded "ethnoids." Her family, studies, ICE, and ministry in Siberia now fill her days.

Mary Hendershott

Mary Hendershott, MA, is an ethnomusicologist with Wycliffe Bible Translators. She currently lives and works in Burkina Faso, West Africa.

Michael T. Heneise

Michael T. Heneise is a classically trained opera baritone and ethnomusicologist. He studied jazz guitar at the Berklee College of Music, has a BME in Choral Conducting from Florida State University, and an MTh in Contextual Missiology from the University of Wales. Focusing on Christ and culture issues among mainly indigenous and marginalized people groups in the Americas, Southeast Asia, and Europe, Michael has partnered with International Ministries of the American Baptist Churches, USA, and its overseas partners in developing worship contextualization as an integral mission practice. He is currently pursuing his PhD at the International Baptist Theological Seminary, Prague, and resides with his wife Neisazonuo Yhome-Heneise in Wynnewood, Pennsylvania. Michael is the son of missionary-theologians who have worked in Haiti, Nicaragua, and Chile.

Mark Hepner

Mark and Carol Hepner started living and working among the Bargam people of Madang province, Papua New Guinea in July 1982. The New Testament was dedicated on July 13, 2002.

Catherine Hodges

Catherine and Rob Hodges are missionaries working with Overseas Missionary Fellowship in Indonesia. Rob is an ethnomusicologist and has worked in this field since the mid-1980s.

Roberta King

Roberta King, PhD, is associate professor of Communication and Ethnomusicology at Fuller Theological Seminary. She directs the program in Global Christian Worship.

James R. Krabill

James R. Krabill, PhD, served for fourteen years as a Bible and church history teacher among independent churches in West Africa. While working with the Harrist Church in southcentral Ivory Coast, he recorded and transcribed over five hundred locally-composed songs in the Dida language. These were compiled into four hymn booklets for use in worship and literacy training and which later became the subject of a PhD dissertation at the University of Birmingham (U.K.). Author of several books, including, *The Hymnody of the Harrist Church* (1995), *A Theology of Mission for Today* (1999), *Does Your Church "Smell" Like Mission?* (2001) and *Is It Insensitive to Share Your Faith?* (2005). James is currently Senior Executive for Global Ministries at the Mennonite Mission Network, in Elkhart, Indiana.

Aretta Loving

Aretta Loving, along with her husband, Ed, serve with Wycliffe Bible Translators. The Lovings were translators with the Awa people of Papua New Guinea. Aretta is the author of *Slices of Life, Devotions and Stories from a Bible Translator.*

Don McCurry

Dr. McCurry, PhD, served with the Presbyterian Mission in Pakistan for 18 years. Upon his return to the United States, he earned his doctorate at Fuller Seminary in the School of World Mission and was invited to stay on and teach. After seven years, he founded a ministry that would enable him to teach as a free-lance teacher wherever he was invited in the world. In this capacity, he has led training programs in various settings in some sixty-five countries. Currently, he has been teaching in Spain and Central Asia.

Paul Neeley

Paul Neeley became seriously involved with music at age twelve, focusing on drums and percussion. He has lived in West Africa off and on for twelve years, working with SIL, and has done music workshops with members of about thirty-five ethnic groups in various parts of Africa. He is also involved with music ministry in parts of Asia and elsewhere. He is a member of Artists in Christian Testimony, International Worship & Arts Network, and Heart Sounds International. He has published two books, over fifty articles, and edits the journal *EthnoDoxology*. He teaches ethnomusicology at two universities and has served as a consultant for various mission agencies. His doctorate, with a focus in African music studies, is forthcoming from the University of Ghana. A few years ago, in conjunction with Prairie Bible College, Paul co-produced two CDs of Celtic Christian music. He has a perpetual interest to know a bit about all musics all over the world, so he is a constant learner. At last count, he had 1,237 favorite types of music.

Linda Neeley

Linda Neeley worked on the Akyode Bible translation and literacy project in Ghana from 1979 until the New Testament was completed and dedicated in December 2001. She continues to have a part in the Old Testament translation in that language and to work on the Translator's Notes project in Wycliffe's International Translation Department in Dallas. She and Paul have two sons.

Von Newcomb

Von Newcomb lives in Central Asia with his wife and three children and heads a ministry focused on ethnodoxology. He spends his time helping talented, unknown artists do new and exciting things for God with all kinds of instruments—both common and bizarre—in a language only a few million people understand.

Bruce Olson

Bruce Olson has dedicated his life to evangelizing the Motilone of Colombia, South America. In 1961, as a nineteen-year-old, he went to live with this then-murderous people. It took several years to win the first Motilone to Christ, but today almost all are Christian. Bruce continues to live with the Motilones. They have joined hands with him in sending missionary teams to non-evangelized peoples in northeast Colombia and western Venezuela. In 2002, Regent University granted Bruce an Honorary Doctor of Divinity Degree for his contribution to missions philosophy and service. A new book, *Bruchko and the Motilone Miracle* (August 2006), picks up where *Bruchko* left off and recounts many of the advances the Motilones have made as a result of Bruce's willingness to follow God's path into the jungles of South America. For more info, see: www.bruceolson.com and www.christianlifemissions.org.

John Oswald

John Oswald with WEC (World Evangelization for Christ) International is an ethnomusicology tutor currently coordinating a multi-media storytelling DVD production, incorporating indigenous music, song, dance, art, and narration. He teaches ethnomusicology in college and cross-cultural training settings in Europe and Asia. After gaining a master's degree in ethnomusicology from the University of London, he researched regional folk music in the Himalayas and has put together a suite of contextual worship song resources. He is married, has two daughters and one son, and enjoys hill walking.

Steve Pierson

Steve Pierson, PhD, gave his life to Christ at the University of Illinois. He served with Greater Europe Mission at the Nordic Bible Institute in Scandinavia and

Eastern Europe from 1976 until 1996. Steve currently teaches at Wheaton College and the College of DuPage. He holds a BS and MS in Music Education from the University of Illinois, an MA in Cross Cultural Communications from Wheaton College, and a PhD in Education from Trinity International University.

Jack Popjes

Canadians Jack and Jo Popjes spent twenty-two years studying the language and translating Scriptures for the Canela people of Brazil. Today, they promote the work of Bible translation as Wycliffe representatives in Canada.

Rodolfo and Beatrice Senn

Rodolfo and Beatrice Senn have worked with Wycliffe Bible Translators since 1987. Rodolfo is Argentinean (all his grandparents immigrated to Argentina from Switzerland in 1937). Beatrice is Swiss.

Richard Shawyer

Dr. Richard Shawyer has served with WEC (World Evangelization for Christ) International as a church planter among the Wolof people of West Africa since 1993. He has a passion to see non-literate oral communicators solidly founded in God's Word, and a national community of believers that expresses itself in ways that are truly Wolof, yet authentically Christian.

Nola Shoemaker

Nola and Jack Shoemaker, with Wycliffe Bible Translators, began working with the Utes in 1986, after finishing a translation project with the Ese Ejja people of Bolivia. Jack grew up in southwest Colorado, worked among the Navajo during high school and college, and knew of the Utes at that time.

Glenn Stallsmith

Glenn and his wife, Sarah, met at Asbury College while studying missions and music. They were drawn to ethnomusicology as their desire grew to use their musical talents to further the Bible translation effort. In 2001 they began their first assignment as ethnomusicologists to the Philippines. Since then they have been helping people understand that God can both speak and sing in their language. Glenn is currently pursuing an MA degree in Ethnomusicology from Bethel University. Glenn and Sarah have three daughters: Catherine, Madeline, and Molly.

Colin and Dot Suggett

Colin and Dot Suggett joined Wycliffe Bible Translators in 1988 and began work in the Turka project in 1993. They have two children, Iris and Lily.

Julie Taylor

Julie Taylor, PhD, followed the Lord's prompting and moved to Africa in 1993, after some twenty years trotting the globe as a concert violinist. She is the coordinator of Anthropology and Ethnomusicology for SIL Africa region, encouraging the development of culturally relevant worship and research among minority language groups. Her training includes the Royal College of Music (London), MA in Ethnomusicology and Intercultural Studies (Wheaton, Illinois), and PhD in Ethnomusicology (Edinburgh). Her primary field research has been in Papua New Guinea and Kenya, and her focus today continues to be music performance and teaching.

Rolly Walter

Rolly Walter and his wife, Robyn, served with Avant Ministries (formerly Gospel Missionary Union) in Bolivia from 1995 to 1997. They currently work in video production at Avant's Málaga Media Center in Spain.

Jeanette Windle

Jeanette Windle and her husband, Marty, served with Avant Ministries (formerly Gospel Missionary Union) in Bolivia from 1985 to 2000, and now reside in southern Florida.

James Ziersch

James Ziersch and his wife, Lydia, began working among the Marakwet people in December 2003. James previously worked as a teacher for fifteen years in Australia, six months in Papua New Guinea, and one year in Kenya's capital, Nairobi. The projected New Testament dedication date of April 2008 is one of the main goals guiding and inspiring the use of Marakwet Christian cultural music.

To contact any of the authors, please send
your email to information@worldofworship.org
and it will be forwarded to the author.

Ethnodoxology in Missions Links

Artists in Christian Testimony
www.ACTinternational.org

International Council of Ethnodoxologists
www.worldofworship.org

EthnoDoxology Journal
http://ethnodoxology.org

Global Consultation on Music and Missions
www.gcommhome.org

Heart Sounds International
www.heart-sounds.org

Wycliffe Bible Translators, Ethnomusicology Dept.
www.wycliffe.org/ethnomusic/home.htm

Global Christian Worship program at Fuller Seminary
www.fuller.edu/swm/conc/gcw.asp

Ethnomusicology Program at Bethel University
http://gs.bethel.edu/musicology

BuildABridge
www.buildabridge.org

Christian Arts Network of Japan
www.japancan.com

Disciple the Nations
www.disciplethenations.org

International Worship & Arts Network, Ethnic Worship Index
www.worship-arts-network.com/ethnic-music-index.html

Greater Europe Mission—Worship Resources
www.worr.org

The Menorah Project
http://members.aol.com/MenorahACT/

Worship from the Nations
http://projects.crossnet.hu/wfn/

Calvin Institute of Christian Worship
http://www.calvin.edu/worship/

Heart Sounds INTERNATIONAL

Heart Sounds International (HSI) sends teams of worship musicians and recording engineers to various nations to:

- record indigenous audio and video projects
- teach on biblical worship
- organize songwriting workshops
- provide technical training
- assist in research of cultural musical forms for appropriate worship expression

HSI installs modest professional audio and video recording studios for ongoing projects to help enable continuing music and video production.

HSI works mostly in West and Central Asia, the Indian Subcontinent, the Middle East and North Africa.

Heart Sounds INTERNATIONAL

PO Box 444
Tyrone, GA 30290
770-631-0432
http://www.heart-sounds.org
info@heart-sounds.org

International Council of Ethnodoxologists

The vision of ICE is that Christians from every culture will have the opportunity to express their faith through their own heart music and arts.

ICE provides:

- **Connections** – through our email forums and conferences, we provide encouragement, prayer support, resources, networking, and mentoring for our associates worldwide.

- **Certification** – recognition for advanced training and experience is now available on two levels:
  - *Certified Missionary Ethnomusicologist*
  - *Ethnomusicology Training Specialist*

- **Clearinghouse** – we have the world's largest online library on the culturally-appropriate use of music and arts in ministry.

"The founding of ICE is a watershed event. With today's groundswell of global worship, there is an unprecedented opportunity to proclaim God's salvation to the nations via culturally appropriate worship and music."
- Dr. Roberta King, Fuller Theological Seminary

Come join us!

www.worldofworship.org

At WFI, we seek to prepare & release worship artists for kingdom impact. Whether it's by reaching the nations through Global Impact Teams, honing creativity through Songwriter's Journey, or connecting people through the Worship Mentors Network, we strive to train the next generation of musicians and artists to engage culture to the glory of God.

Visit www.worshipfoundations.com for more information on how you can join us in seeing Revelation 7:9-10 fulfilled.

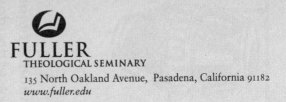